Minority Women and Agency in Iran

This book illuminates the underexamined histories and lived experiences of Bahá'í women in Iran, tracing their engagement with structures of exclusion, resistance, and social transformation from the nineteenth century to the present. Situating these narratives within the longue durée of Iranian sociopolitical change, the book explores how religious marginalization and gendered inequality intersect to shape both constraints and possibilities for agency.

Combining historical analysis with close attention to lived experience, this study foregrounds voices that have remained largely absent from both nationalist historiography and dominant feminist accounts. In doing so, it highlights how Bahá'í women have negotiated complex forms of belonging while contributing to broader processes of social and political change, including those reflected in the contemporary Woman, Life, Freedom movement.

By placing these experiences in dialogue with debates on social movements, minority rights, and political participation, the book offers a nuanced rethinking of agency under conditions of constraint. Both analytically rigorous and accessible, this work will engage scholars of gender and Middle Eastern studies while inviting a wider readership to reconsider the role of marginalized actors in shaping modern Iran.

Raha Sabet Sarvestany is a postdoctoral researcher and lecturer in the Department of Gender Studies at Åbo Akademi University, Finland. She holds a PhD in Women's Studies and conducts research on gender, religion, minority rights, and authoritarianism, with a particular focus on Iran and the Bahá'í community. Her scholarship examines the intersections of religion, gender, and power, with particular attention to social movements, minority experiences, and political repression in authoritarian contexts.

Routledge Advances in Minority Studies

Series Editors:

Stavroula Pipyrou *is a Senior Lecturer in Social Anthropology at the University of St Andrews, UK, and Founding Director of the cross-disciplinary Centre for Minorities Research (CMR). She has published widely on minority politics, governance, and civil society in Italy and Greece.*

Kyriaki Topidi *is Head of the Research Cluster on Culture and Diversity and a Senior Researcher at the European Centre for Minority Issues, Germany. Her research interests focus on diversity management, minority protection rights and mechanisms, with a special interest in religion, and human rights law. She has published extensively on these and related areas.*

Routledge Advances in Minority Studies (RAMS) provides a platform for outstanding state-of-the-art research on interdisciplinary and intersectional understandings of minorities, globally. Monographs and edited volumes in the series advance scholarly and practitioner insights from Anthropology, Law, Politics, Sociology, History and beyond. The series foregrounds pluralism and diversity of both authors and subjects of study, with a particular focus on emerging fields and marginalized voices.

Under the editorial supervision of Dr Stavroula Pipyrou and Dr Kyriaki Topidi, the series will be a primary source for students, scholars and practitioners in minority studies while presenting authors with a valuable means to reach a wide and growing readership.

Titles in the series:

Minorities, Scarcity and Conflict
Edited by Antonio Montañés Jimenez, Camila Ferreira Marinelli, and Stavroula Pipyrou

Minority Women, Rights, and Intersectionality
Agency, Power, and Participation
Edited by Alexandra Cosima Budabin, Jody Metcalfe and Shilpi Pandey

Minorities, Identity and Intermarriage
A European Perspective
Edited by Karolina Lendák-Kabók and Martin Klatt

Minority Women and Agency in Iran
The Unyielding Voices of the Bahá'í Community
Raha Sabet Sarvestany

For more information about this series, please visit: https://www.routledge.com/Routledge-Advances-in-Minority-Studies/book-series/RAIMS

Minority Women and Agency in Iran

The Unyielding Voices of the Bahá'í Community

Raha Sabet Sarvestany

Routledge
Taylor & Francis Group
LONDON AND NEW YORK

First published 2027
by Routledge
4 Park Square, Milton Park, Abingdon, Oxon OX14 4RN

and by Routledge
605 Third Avenue, New York, NY 10158

Routledge is an imprint of the Taylor & Francis Group, an informa business

British Library Cataloguing-in-Publication Data
A catalogue record for this book is available from the British Library

ISBN: 978-1-032-93969-8 (hbk)
ISBN: 978-1-032-93734-2 (pbk)
ISBN: 978-1-003-56737-0 (ebk)

DOI: 10.4324/9781003567370

Typeset in Times New Roman
by Apex CoVantage, LLC

Contents

Preface: The Journey That Led to This Book

Almost 200 years ago, the Bahá'í faith emerged in Iran, articulating a transformative spiritual and social vision for humanity. This new religious movement introduced a new horizon of moral and social maturity grounded in the belief that human beings possess the collective capacity to construct a more just, peaceful, and unified civilization. Central to its teachings were principles such as universal education, the independent investigation of truth, the oneness of humankind, and in particular, the equality of women and men, with special emphasis on the education and development of women in all aspect of the life as a priority.

These ideas spread rapidly among segments of Iranian society who were dissatisfied with prevailing corruption, social injustice, and the stagnation of existing institutions. For many, the Bahá'í teachings generated both hope and aspiration for the possibility of an alternative social order. At the same time, however, they provoked deep anxiety and hostility among some of the political authorities and religious leaders, particularly Muslim, who perceived this emerging movement as a challenge to established power structures and doctrinal authority.

The former paragraphs draw on the extensive body of Bahá'í literature written by Bahá'í scholars for both academic and general audiences. What has motivated me to contribute to this book is the desire to build upon this existing scholarship through the lens of my own lived experience as a Bahá'í woman in post-revolutionary Iran. I aim to illustrate what it means to belong to an unrecognized religious minority and, more specifically, to be a woman within that context.

I was born and raised in a Bahá'í family and community in Shiraz, where my identity was deeply shaped by Bahá'í values and communal life. My childhood coincided with the early years of the Islamic Revolution, when the Islamic courts initiated widespread arrests, executions, confiscation of property, and raids on Bahá'í homes. Many of my earliest memories are marked by standing at the gates of Adelabad Prison, through harsh winters and intense summers, waiting to visit my uncle and grandfather. I witnessed how prison guards routinely humiliated and psychologically intimidated Bahá'ís in an effort to break their spirits before visits. I also lived through the execution of ten Bahá'í women, including my aunt, who was in her twenties at the time. Growing up in such an environment, I did not yet fully understand the Bahá'í teachings or administrative structures, but I clearly saw how members of my family were prepared to sacrifice their lives for their faith.

My first direct encounter with the brutality of discrimination occurred when I was only five years old. Islamic guards raided our home, confiscating all books, pictures, and objects that signified our Bahá'í identity. Before leaving, they informed my father that he was required to present himself to the Islamic court the following day. I do not know what went through my parents' minds that night, but I vividly remember my father embracing my sister and me, saying goodbye in a way that felt unfamiliar and unsettling. I did not yet understand that many Bahá'ís were being arrested, kidnapped, or killed during those years. I only sensed that something was deeply different. When my father finally returned home that night, it felt like a celebration for my mother, my sister, and me, simply because he had come back alive.

My second formative experience occurred when our family was forced to relocate from Haft-Tappeh, a town near Ahvaz, to Shiraz due to the Iran–Iraq War. I was about 7 years old. One morning, all of our relatives gathered at my grandfather's house for breakfast because he had been ordered to report to the Islamic court. That was the last day we saw him. At the time, I could not comprehend why my aunts, uncles, cousins, and grandmother prayed together with such intensity after the meal. Yet even as a child, I could sense that something irreversible was about to happen.

Gradually, I learned that each time the telephone rang, my family braced itself for distressing news. State media regularly reported the execution of Bahá'ís across different cities in Iran. One day, a call confirmed that my grandfather had died in prison only a few days after the execution of sixteen Bahá'ís in Shiraz. His death did not come as a complete shock: during our final visit, he was already confined to a wheelchair, severely ill, and deprived of adequate medical care. He died at the age of 73. The prison authorities recorded the cause of death as a heart attack. Yet, for years, I have carried the lingering question of whether neglect, or even suffocation, may have contributed while he lay unconscious. Although international pressure eventually led the Islamic Republic to slow the pace of executions, persecution did not end. Instead, it evolved into new forms of exclusion, surveillance, and systematic deprivation.

In this environment, I gradually learned the value of human life, the meaning of belonging to the Bahá'í community, and the forms of resilience required to endure hardship. All of this shaped my identity organically, long before I was 8 years old. I began to recognize how different my life was from that of my classmates. My thoughts and conversations did not resemble theirs. While other children went home after school, I often accompanied my family to the prison to visit my grandfather and uncle, finishing my homework while waiting at the prison gates. I also accompanied my parents to the Islamic court whenever they were summoned to follow up on the cases of our loved ones. I attended memorial gatherings for Bahá'ís executed in Shiraz.

Yet I could not speak about any of these experiences at school. I remained silent, unable to share what I had witnessed or learned. Instead, I listened quietly as my classmates spoke about what seemed like ordinary childhood concerns. My teachers, for their part, never asked how I felt or what I was going through. I was expected to perform well educationally regardless of the extraordinary pressures that defined my life outside the classroom. I was 9 years old when my teacher linked the mathematical definition of a right triangle to the Islamic concept of the "Promised One" and instructed the entire class to stand in reverence for a ritual anticipating his future arrival to establish Islamic rule across the world. I refused. When questioned, I answered honestly: according to Bahá'í teachings, the Promised One has already come. My response provoked anger. I was expelled from the classroom and soon dismissed from the school altogether.

My parents tried repeatedly to persuade the principal and teacher to readmit me. Eventually, I was forced to write a letter promising to "respect" the teacher and to conceal my beliefs. Although I returned to school, nothing felt the same. Despite being one of the highest-performing students and contributing to the improvement of the school's national ranking, I was never publicly acknowledged. Instead, the student who ranked second was celebrated, while I was privately informed that no Bahá'í could receive public recognition.

This pattern persisted throughout middle and high school. My parents continually reminded me that the true value lay in learning itself, not in public praise. Their words became a steady source of grounding through each new challenge. When the time came to sit for the national university entrance examination, the principal spoke candidly to my parents: "Your daughter cannot enter university because she is a Bahá'í. If she writes that she is Muslim, she may continue, and both she and the school will benefit. Tell her to keep her faith in her heart." My parents remained silent, entrusting the decision to me. By the age of 18, I had already witnessed years of persecution: our home repeatedly raided; my father, uncle, and grandfather arrested; my young aunt executed alongside nine other Bahá'í women; my grandfather dying in prison due to lack of medical care; and my father dismissed from his job solely because of his faith. Faced with this choice, I decided to remain truthful. I refused to lie.

My experience of being denied access to higher education reflects the broader reality facing Bahá'í youth in Iran to this day. In response to systematic exclusion in the early 1980s, the Bahá'í community established an underground higher-education system so that Bahá'í students could at least pursue studies up to the bachelor's level. I continued my education through this system, the Bahá'í Institute for Higher Education (BIHE). Within this covert educational network, I completed both my bachelor's and master's degrees, becoming an independent and self-directed learner shaped by both necessity and conviction. Later, I was invited to join the faculty. By the age of 24, I had been appointed to the educational board, an immense responsibility, and a profound milestone, given the severe pressures and risks under which we worked.

Unable to pursue formal employment as a Bahá'í graduate in Iran, I devoted myself to children's education and women's empowerment across the country. I later joined a human rights NGO, and in 2006, under Ahmadinejad's increasingly fundamentalist state, I was arrested for this humanitarian work. My identity as a Bahá'í intensified the severity of the persecution I faced, and I was sentenced to four years of solitary confinement. Solitary confinement was initially unbearable. Yet I discovered resilience in an inner moral and spiritual conviction shaped by faith and a profound longing for freedom. I fought simply for the right to have a book, and eventually permission was granted. Over time, I obtained paper and a pen. In that confined space, I began writing academic reflections and articles, transforming isolation into a site of intellectual inquiry and creation. Those years taught me that resilience, discipline, and curiosity are not privileges; they are lifelines. Even while my body was imprisoned, I learned that freedom of thought could not be contained.

Upon my release in 2010, I confronted a new dilemma: remaining in Iran meant the risk of re-arrest. I made the difficult decision to leave, one I have never entirely reconciled with emotionally. I continued my studies abroad, completing a second master's degree in India and later a PhD in Women's Studies, focusing on agency and resilience, concepts I had both examined academically and lived personally. Despite years of academic work, I was unable to secure employment and returned to Iran in 2017. Although I held a PhD and extensive teaching experience, I was barred from all professional opportunities because of my faith and my record as a political prisoner. It was only through the support of Scholars at Risk (SAR) that I was able to continue my academic path. In 2020, SAR facilitated visiting researcher position at the University of Oslo. Sitting in that office for the first time, I wept: I was finally able to study, write, teach, and speak without fear.

Yet freedom did not erase struggle; it merely transformed it. I had to navigate unfamiliar academic systems, revalidate my credentials, and rebuild a scholarly record that had been deliberately erased through censorship in Iran. I repeated pedagogical and supervision trainings to meet European standards, reconstructed my publication portfolio, and learned once again how to situate myself within new academic landscapes. Today, I continued this journey at Åbo Akademi University, where I have been awarded funding to pursue two further years of postdoctoral research. Yet the future remains uncertain. As global political dynamics become increasingly unstable, the circumstances of forcibly displaced scholars from certain regions risk slipping from public concern. I do not know whether these years of struggle will ultimately open a path to a position through which I can meaningfully serve humanity, or whether I may one day be compelled to return to my country.

For me, writing this book is not only an intellectual project but also an ethical responsibility to future generations. It provides a space to translate lived experience into knowledge, and to intervene in wider scholarly and public debates concerning injustice, faith, gender, and human dignity. Although the narrative is written in the first person, it speaks to experiences shared by many, not only Bahá'í women in Iran, nor even Iranian women more broadly, but individuals across diverse contexts who have grown up under conditions of marginalization and exclusion. This book seeks to connect theory with lived reality. More broadly, it examines how faith, culture, history, and political structures intersect to shape subjectivity from the earliest stages of life. These socially constructed identities, frequently imposed rather than chosen, come to organize one's access to rights, resources, and recognition. At the same time, the narrative foregrounds the persistent capacity for human action: what contemporary minority and feminist theorists conceptualize as agency and resilience.

The Enduring Bahá'í Community

Since 1979, the social identity of the Bahá'í community in Iran has been shaped by persistent hardship, discrimination, and systematic exclusion, policies intentionally designed by the Islamic Republic to remove the Bahá'ís from Iranian society. Yet the community's social identity has also been formed through resilience and the active agency of its members, who have continually sought ways to educate, organize, and sustain communal life despite repression. This dynamic distinguishes the experience of Bahá'ís in Iran from that of Bahá'í communities elsewhere. Over the past four decades, these challenges have also profoundly influenced the global Bahá'í community, which has increasingly acted as an advocate for Iranian Bahá'ís. Through public campaigns, diplomatic engagement, and collaboration with international human rights organizations and governments, global Bahá'ís have worked to secure recognition, visibility, and protection for their Iranian co-religionists. Although such efforts have not ended persecution, they have at times reduced their severity and ensured that abuses are documented and contested.

However, recent developments, including the Woman, Life, Freedom movement, have coincided with renewed and intensified discrimination against Bahá'ís, often without restraint and despite global attention. This book argues that the self-determination of an unrecognized religious minority, living under an authoritarian regime, can generate new understandings of key social and ethical concepts. In the case of the Bahá'í community in Iran, these understandings emerge from the teachings of the Bahá'í Faith itself, which not only differ from dominant political and religious discourses but also produce distinctive forms of practice. The narratives presented here demonstrate how the agency and resilience of Iranian Bahá'ís articulate alternative meanings of freedom, justice, service, power, education, cooperation, and unity.

These are not framed merely as strategies of resistance to oppression; rather, they function as the foundations for imagining and constructing new patterns of community life.

The selective narratives of Bahá'í women, both before and after the Islamic Revolution, represent only a fraction of the many accounts that document how these women reclaim agency in the face of authoritarian repression. Grounded in faith and enacted during periods of profound hardship, their experiences extend ongoing feminist debates on faith-based agency and resilience while contributing a distinct analytical perspective to these discussions. These narratives do not focus on challenging patriarchy within religion; rather, they demonstrate how the Bahá'í Faith itself becomes a source of agency for breaking patriarchal structures and prejudice. They illustrate how Bahá'í teachings provide the foundational principles for self-determination, activism, and the building of modern and democratic forms of community and society, even under authoritarian rule. However, these narratives do not suggest that the wider sociopolitical changes in Iran have had no effect. Rather, they illustrate how the Bahá'í community and Iranian society have increasingly learned from one another. What once appeared as two separate trajectories now intersect more than ever, as prolonged oppression and life under an authoritarian regime have generated new forms of solidarity and shared struggle. Across successive social movements, especially among marginalized and minority groups, this mutual learning has strengthened collective efforts to imagine and work toward change.

This book advances a multilayered argument about Otherness, agency, and resistance in contemporary Iran, and it intervenes directly in debates within minority studies, feminist theory, and scholarship on agency and resilience. I contend that the production of Otherness has not only fragmented Iranian society but has been systematically mobilized by those in power as a mechanism of governance, silencing dissenting voices and disciplining communities that do not conform to the Islamic state narrative. Against this backdrop, I argue that practices of resistance among minorities, and particularly among Bahá'í women, both reflect and reshape evolving understandings of collective agency and intersectional liberation.

To develop this argument, the book integrates intersectionality, feminist thought, theories of agency and structure, social identity theory, and resilience studies into an interdisciplinary analytical framework capable of capturing the layered dynamics of marginalization and resistance. It traces the relationship between recurring political crises within the Islamic Republic and the intensification of persecution targeting the Bahá'í community, with particular attention to the period following the Woman, Life, Freedom movement. By situating Bahá'í women's epistemic and embodied agency within this broader sociopolitical landscape, the book demonstrates how their commitments to care, education, moral service, and nonconfrontational advocacy contribute to a pluralistic vision of justice and solidarity in Iran.

I further argue that engaging Bahá'í theological concepts alongside intersectional feminist theory challenges dominant secular paradigms of resistance and offers a decolonial reading of agency. Through what I term the "Paradox of Suppressed Alternatives (PSA)," the book advances the claim that authoritarian repression functions as a tacit acknowledgment of the transformative potential posed by marginalized communities. The agency of Bahá'í women thus emerges not merely as reactive but as constitutive: a blueprint for spiritually grounded, ethically rooted, and transnationally visible forms of resistance that unsettle conventional hierarchies of power.

Ultimately, the book contends that politically marginalized women are not only targets of repression but also theorists of transformation. By centering faith-informed epistemologies and lived experience, it expands feminist vocabularies of agency and brings into focus forms of resistance too often dismissed as apolitical or invisible. In a global moment marked by escalating authoritarianism and shrinking democratic space, the narratives and conceptual frameworks developed here operate both as critique and as guide, inviting a reimagining of justice through intertwined logics of faith, care, resilience, and collective responsibility.

AI-assisted tools, including Grammarly, were used for language editing and structural clarity. The author retained full responsibility for the intellectual content of the book.

Introduction

Beyond the Veil: The Role of the "Other" in Iranian Society Since the Islamic Revolution

Introduction

This chapter examines how Otherness is produced, governed, and contested in contemporary Iran and how marginalized communities generate alternative forms of agency under authoritarian rule. It argues that the construction of Otherness functions not merely as a social condition but as a deliberate technology of governance, one that fragments society, disciplines nonconforming populations, and suppresses dissenting moral and political imaginaries. Against this backdrop, the practices of marginalized groups reveal how agency can be exercised collectively, ethically, and relationally, even in contexts defined by systematic exclusion.

Engaging critically with the concept of "minority," this study interrogates how minority status is not merely descriptive but actively constitutive of social hierarchies. The categorization of groups as minorities, along with the ranking, prioritization, or differentiation among them, reinforces binary modes of belonging and exclusion. Such frameworks not only deepen divisions between dominant and marginalized populations but also reproduce cultures of difference, preconception, and competition both within and across minority communities themselves. By foregrounding this critique, the chapter challenges static and hierarchical understandings of minorityhood and instead examines how Otherness is produced, managed, and contested as part of broader mechanisms of authoritarian governance.

Based on my observations and life experience, and drawing on Asef Bayat's analysis of post-revolutionary social control, the intricate mosaic of societal diversity in Iranian society has been systematically fragmented since the Islamic Revolution, which sought to impose an Islamic framework across all aspects of life (Bayat 2013). The imposition of the Islamic framework has reshaped societal diversity, fragmenting it into isolated compartments and leading to growing segregation and disengagement among communities, groups, and individuals.

The Islamic Republic's promotion of exclusionary narratives has deepened cultural segregation and social fragmentation in Iran. The state's ideological project has destabilized Iran's historically plural social fabric, comprising

DOI: 10.4324/9781003567370-1

diverse ethnic, linguistic, cultural, and religious communities, including Arabs, Kurds, Lors, Baluchis, Bahá'ís, Christians, Jews, and Sufi/Dervish groups. In narrowing the space for diversity and enforcing ideological conformity, authoritarian governance has weakened everyday social life and eroded the conditions necessary for a just and inclusive public sphere. In this sense, the erosion of diversity ultimately constrains the prospects for national cohesion and for meaningful political or social transformation. Yet the mass uprising following the state-sanctioned killing of Mahsa Jina Amini[1] complicates this path. It reveals that beneath the imposed divisions lies a latent collective will, across boundaries of ethnicity, religion, and gender, capable of resisting fragmentation and envisioning a more inclusive and unified society.[2]

Dividing the Nation: State Power, Identity Politics, and the "Us vs. Them" Paradigm

The establishment of the Islamic Republic of Iran in 1979, under the leadership of Ayatollah Khomeini, marked the introduction of a regime grounded in Shia Islamic law and tradition. This theocratic government has employed judicial and police powers to enforce religious doctrines, positioning non-Shia Muslims as subordinate within the social and political hierarchy (Chehabi 1991; Iran Human Rights Documentation Center 2022; Dadpour 2025). This approach, rooted in their interpretation of Islamic laws that serve to advance their social and economic securities within Iran, represents the initial steps in cultivating a societal sense of otherness. As scholars such as Foucault (1978), Levinas (1969), and more recent theorists including Bhabha (2004), Ahmed (2000), and Mbembe (2003) argue, otherness is not a natural condition but a social and political construction that marks certain groups as different, threatening, or less deserving of protection.

Drawing on Hannah Arendt's analysis of totalitarianism, I argue that the creation of a societal "other" within the Islamic Republic of Iran reflects key characteristics of totalitarian regimes. These include the enforcement of rigid ideological divisions, the marginalization of minority groups, and the strategic deployment of state power to suppress dissent and manufacture conformity (Arendt 1951). Within this framework, the Iranian societal "other" can be understood through five distinct but interrelated categories: (1) the marginalization of religious minorities, (2) gender-based exclusion, (3) ethnic

1 Her death became a symbol of resistance against gender-based oppression and state control, particularly targeting women's rights. The incident triggered massive demonstrations under the slogan "Woman, Life, Freedom," highlighting demands for personal freedoms, gender equality, and broader political reforms in Iran. Further elaboration regarding this topic is provided in various chapters throughout the book.

2 https://www.omct.org/en/resources/statements/iran-a-year-after-mahsa-aminis-death-human-rights-are-still-under-attack

fragmentation and suppression, (4) the repression of political dissent, and (5) the cultural construction of otherness. These forms of exclusion reinforce one another, constituting a multifaceted system that delegitimizes those outside the regime's narrow definition of belonging.

The Marginalization of Religious Minorities

Since the Islamic Revolution, Iran's constitution has officially recognized only three religious minorities: Christians, Jews, and Zoroastrians.[3] Other groups including Sunni Muslims, despite being part of the global Muslim majority are not classified as religious minorities in the constitution due to their inclusion within Islam, though they remain a minority within Shia-dominated Iran. Unrecognized groups such as Bahá'ís, Yarsanis (Ahl-e Haqq), Mandaeans, Hindus, Buddhists, and others are denied constitutional protection and basic civil rights, and face systemic discrimination and persecution.[4] The Yarsanis (Ahl-e Haqq),[5] primarily Kurdish, are labeled heretical and pressured to identify as Muslims. Sunni Muslims, particularly in Sistan and Baluchistan, Kurdistan, and Khuzestan, face political and social marginalization.[6] Mandaeans,[7] an ancient Gnostic community in southwestern Iran, suffer severe discrimination, forcing many to flee. Christian converts from Islam are punished for apostasy, facing imprisonment or death.[8] Sufi Muslims, especially the Gonabadi Order,[9] endure arrests and attacks on their worship practices.[10] Nontraditional Zoroastrian revivalists and Kakai (Shabak) groups are viewed with suspicion and are often forced to hide their faith.[11] These minorities face restrictions in education, employment, and political representation, exacerbated

3 These groups are granted certain rights under **Article 13** of the Constitution, which states, "*Zoroastrians, Jews, and Christians are the only recognized religious minorities, who, within the limits of the law, are free to perform their religious rites and ceremonies, and to act according to their own canon in matters of personal affairs and religious education.*"

4 https://www.state.gov/reports/2023-report-on-international-religious-freedom/iran/

5 https://oraltradition.org/the-religious-textual-heritage-of-the-yarsan-ahl-e-haqq/

6 https://www.washingtoninstitute.org/policy-analysis/sunnis-iran-protesting-against-decades-discrimination-and-repression, https://www.state.gov/reports/2023-report-on-international-religious-freedom/iran/

7 https://iranwire.com/en/features/67646/

8 https://www.asianews.it/news-en/Iran,-a-Christian-convert-to-face-death-penalty-for-apostasy-2972.html

9 Sufi Muslims, especially the Gonabadi Order, represent a mystical dimension of Islam that emphasizes personal spiritual experience, meditation, and devotion to God beyond formalistic or legalistic practices. The Gonabadi Order is the largest Sufi tariqa in Iran, tracing its lineage through centuries of spiritual leadership and emphasizing ethical conduct, humility, and the pursuit of inner knowledge.

10 https://www.europarl.europa.eu/meetdocs/2009_2014/documents/d-ir/dv/hr_violations_dervish/hr_violations_dervishes.pdf

11 https://er.ceres.rub.de/index.php/ER/article/view/11525/11272

by accusations of heresy or threats to national security (Sanasarian 2000; Sajoo 2014; Mahmood 2016).

In Iran, the Bahá'í community is not only denied recognition as a religious minority but is also explicitly excluded from any form of legal protection. Ayatollah Ruhollah Khomeini, during his time in Paris in 1978, made it clear that Bahá'í citizens would not be granted civil rights (Cockroft 1979; Zabihi-Moghaddam 2016).[12] Prominent Shiite clergymen attacked the Bahá'ís from the pulpit and in the media, labeling them as "enemies of Islam," "corrupted on earth," "foreign spies," and stating that "their blood deserves to be shed" (Martin 1979, 31). The Bahá'ís have been branded as heretics and accused of espionage for foreign governments, which has resulted in their exclusion from education and employment.

Bahá'ís faced a range of abuses, including physical assaults, confiscation, and destruction of property, abductions and sexual violence, public humiliation, and the destruction of homes, cemeteries, and holy sites. Additionally, Bahá'í prisoners endured torture, and relentless attempts were made to force Bahá'í to renounce their faith. International pressure led the Iranian government to halt the execution of Bahá'ís in the 1980s. However, authorities implemented a new strategy aimed at suppressing the Bahá'í community across all areas of life. A 1991 policy memorandum titled *The Bahá'í Question*, signed by Supreme Leader Ayatollah Ali Khamenei, called for the social mobility of the Bahá'ís to be "blocked," intending to dismantle the community as a viable entity in Iran. This memorandum even extended the policy of persecution to influence actions against Bahá'ís beyond Iran's borders (Bahá'í International Community 2023).[13] Taken together, these systematic strategies have worked to construct and normalize a rigid "us versus them" divide, in which the Islamic Republic and its ideologically loyal insiders constitute the legitimate "us," while Bahá'ís, alongside others who fall outside the state's doctrinal framework, are positioned as suspect outsiders. This division had even broken familial relationships, severing ties between Bahá'í and Muslim kinship, some of whom had been united through marriage before the Islamic Revolution. Therefore, the impact extends beyond the public sphere,

12 Martin, D. (1979). *The Persecution of the Bahá'ís in Iran*. Seven Days, 31. (Interview from December 1978, published in the February 23, 1979, issue of *Seven Days*).

13 The 1991 policy memorandum, titled *The Bahá'í Question*, is one of the most notorious documents exposing the systematic, state-endorsed persecution of the Bahá'í community in Iran over the past three decades. This directive, signed by Iran's Supreme Leader Ayatollah Ali Khamenei, instructs authorities to block the social and economic progress of Bahá'ís. Specifically, it mandates the expulsion of Bahá'í students from universities once their faith is known and falsely accuses Bahá'ís of political and espionage activities. To counter the perceived threat, Iranian propaganda institutions are directed to undermine the Bahá'í community's image. The policy also calls for denying Bahá'ís access to employment and positions of influence, with a further goal to "confront and destroy" their cultural presence internationally. This has to go into the main text body.

infiltrating and transforming the private realm as well. A personal example of this division can be seen in my family's history, where the Islamic Revolution's impact fractured familial ties along religious lines, a situation that reflects broader patterns of division within Iranian society.[14]

Gender-Based Exclusion

The legal frameworks in the Islamic Republic of Iran, which prioritize Shia Islam, not only marginalize religious minorities but also systematically exclude women by enforcing laws grounded in specific religious interpretations of gender, clothing, and women's rights, all of which serve the interests of a totalitarian ideology. These frameworks institutionalize discrimination, embedding unequal treatment into the state's very structure (Mojab 2001; Mahdavi 2017). The regime has entrenched gender inequality by codifying discriminatory laws within its legal system (Badran 2009), particularly those related to marriage, divorce, inheritance, and personal freedoms, including education, sports, employment, and the right to travel abroad, among others. Among all, the mandatory hijab law serves both as a symbolic and practical tool for regulating women's bodies, positioning them as subjects to male-dominated authority under the pretext of religious morality (Yeganeh 2001). The regulation of women's dress has often been interpreted as emblematic of broader mechanisms of social and political control, in which women are constructed as carriers of family honor and cultural authenticity, thereby constraining their visibility and agency in public life. Within this framework, heightened surveillance of women's bodies by both the state and society reinforces patriarchal structures and institutionalized gender hierarchies (Afary 2009; Zaynab 2015). At the same time, however, a growing body of scholarship cautions against reading dress regulation solely through the lens of

14 A personal example of this division is drawn from my own family history. My grandfather, a Bahá'í, married a Muslim woman, and for a time, the two families maintained a relatively cordial relationship, despite occasional tensions among some members. However, after the Islamic Revolution, I witnessed the devastating impact of the regime's division strategies. Extremist members of the Muslim family burned my aunt's house, prompting her relocation from Sarvestan to Shiraz. While there were rumors suggesting that some Muslim relatives from my grandmother's side may have been involved, I refrain from making any judgments regarding their roles. The effects of the political and social changes, however, became tragically apparent when my grandfather was imprisoned and passed away in custody (https://www.iranrights.org/memorial/story/83027/ahmad-ali-sabet-sarvestani, https://iranbahaipersecution.bic.org/archive/ahmad-ali-sabet-sarvestani-died-after-his-transfer-prison-hospital-shiraz-30th-june-1983). Following this, the rift between the families deepened, with my grandmother's relatives severing all ties with her and the rest of the Bahá'í side of the family. This experience is not unique to my family but is emblematic of a broader trend observed in Bahá'í families with Muslim relatives, where the familial bonds were often fractured due to the politicized divisions of the post-revolutionary period.

domination. Scholars such as Mahmood and Göle argue that forms of modest dress can also function as sites of negotiated agency, enabling some women to express religious conviction, cultivate moral subjectivity, or claim participation in public life on their own terms. From this perspective, veiling does not necessarily negate autonomy; rather, it reveals how women may appropriate and reinterpret normative expectations in ways that complicate liberal assumptions about freedom, visibility, and resistance (Mahmood 2005; Göle 2011). These debates underscore that practices surrounding dress are neither uniformly oppressive nor uniformly emancipatory but are embedded in complex fields of power, meaning, and negotiation.

The exclusion of women from equal participation in key sectors, such as politics, the judiciary, and the military, further entrenches their position as the societal "other," solidifying their marginalization within both the public and private spheres. This exclusion is not a mere byproduct of cultural and religious norms but a deliberate and systemic strategy reinforced by state-driven narratives that frame women as the bearers of tradition and moral virtue (Sabet Sarvestany 2023 and 2025). These gendered roles, sanctioned by the state, function not only to perpetuate patriarchal dominance but also to justify the continued disenfranchisement of women from positions of power and decision-making authority (Moghadam 2003). This ideological framework seeks to confine women to prescribed domestic and reproductive roles, effectively erasing their political agency (Arat 1994). By institutionalizing such roles, the regime ensures that women's subordination becomes a structural feature of governance and societal norms (Charrad 2001).

However, the "othering" of women in Iran extends beyond gender alone, intertwining with other axes of marginalization such as class, ethnicity, and religion. Women from minority groups, particularly those of Kurdish, Baluchi, Arab, Sunni, and Bahá'í backgrounds, face a compounded form of discrimination that uniquely positions them at the intersection of multiple oppressive systems.[15] These women experience exclusion not only on the basis of their gender but also because of their ethnic or religious identities, which the state actively seeks to suppress or erase. This intersectional marginalization exposes the multifaceted nature of exclusion in the Islamic Republic of Iran, where women's social roles and political agency are shaped and constrained by overlapping layers of oppression. As such, the exclusion of women cannot be understood in isolation but must be seen as part of a broader strategy of societal control and division, aimed at maintaining a hegemonic, patriarchal order. Through constitutional hierarchies, security discourses, and

15 https://civilica.com/note/3292/ Article 20 of the Constitution: Article 20 emphasizes that all citizens of the nation, both women and men, are equally under the protection of the law and enjoy all human, political, economic, social, and cultural rights in accordance with Islamic criteria (translated from Persian into English).

state-controlled education and media, the Islamic Republic constructs an official narrative of authentic Iranian-Islamic identity against which minorities are measured and disciplined. Ethnic and religious groups are frequently recast as culturally incomplete, politically unreliable, or potentially subversive, particularly when their histories, practices, or transnational connections do not easily fit the state's ideological template. This process does not merely register difference; it works to normalize inequality by determining who may legitimately belong, who must assimilate, and who remains permanently suspect. In this sense, identity becomes a central instrument of governance, through which authoritarian power shapes social imagination, circumscribes citizenship, and limits the possibilities for pluralistic coexistence.

The systematic targeting of Bahá'í women in Iran exemplifies the intersectional discrimination embedded in the regime's policies, which combine both gender-based and religious marginalization with processes of othering. As experts have documented,[16] Bahá'í women face a range of state-driven violations, including arrests, enforced disappearances, raids on homes, confiscation of personal belongings, limitations on freedom of movement, and prolonged deprivation of liberty. These practices disproportionately affect Bahá'í women, who comprise two-thirds of all Bahá'í prisoners in Iran,[17] with many detained without due process and their whereabouts often remaining unknown. According to United Nations experts (United Nations Office of the High Commissioner for Human Rights 2024), the recent surge in targeting Bahá'í women represents an alarming intensification of exclusionary practices, further entrenching their marginalization from public life and subjecting them to intersecting social, economic, and intellectual disadvantages. Systemic barriers, such as the denial of access to higher education and employment opportunities, severely limit the potential of Bahá'í women, with these restrictions beginning in childhood and persisting throughout their lives. These limitations are enforced solely due to their religious beliefs, effectively erasing the contributions that Bahá'í women could otherwise make to Iranian society (United Nations Office of the High Commissioner for Human Rights 2024).

Moreover, the use of vague and ambiguously defined accusations, such as "threats to national security" or "propaganda against the state," illustrates the

16 The experts: Mai Sato, special rapporteur on the situation of human rights in the Islamic Republic of Iran; Nazila Ghanea, special rapporteur on freedom of religion or belief United Nations (2024, December 23). *Iran: Experts alarmed at systematic targeting of Bahá'í women*. Retrieved from https://www.ohchr.org/en/press-releases/2024/12/iran-experts-alarmed-systematic-targeting-bahai-women

17 Since early March 2024, an alarming 72 out of 93 Bahá'ís summoned to court or prison – over three quarters – have been women. https://reliefweb.int/report/iran-islamic-republic/iran-experts-alarmed-systematic-targeting-bahai-women

regime's strategic employment of ideological hegemony[18] (Gramsci 1971) to suppress the Bahá'í community's peaceful exercise of fundamental rights, including freedom of religion, expression, and political participation. The criminalization of these basic rights creates a chilling effect, not only for Bahá'í women but for the entire Bahá'í community in Iran, stifling their ability to live with self-respect and actively participate in society. Intersectional feminist theory, when applied to this context, underscores how the Iranian regime's practices of exclusion and repression while simultaneously operating through processes of othering that construct Bahá'í women, and the Bahá'í community more broadly, as fundamentally outside the boundaries of the national, religious, and moral order.

Ethnic Fragmentation and Suppression

Ethnic fragmentation in Iran is deeply rooted in its complex sociopolitical history, cultural diversity, and state policies that have systematically marginalized non-Farsi speaking ethnic groups. As Mohammadpour and Soleimani (2021) argue, the Iranian state functions within an "ethno-theocratic" framework, which reinforces this marginalization through assimilatory and silencing strategies, further entrenching patterns of ethnic division and exclusion. Despite Iran's multi-ethnic composition, including significant Kurdish, Turk, Baluch, Lurs, Turkmen, and Arab populations, the central government has consistently pursued assimilationist policies aimed at homogenizing the nation's identity under Persian language and Shia Islamic religion hegemony (Aghajanian and Merat 2020). These policies have fostered an environment of exclusion and repression, further deepening ethnic divisions. The Kurdish population, primarily located in the northwest provinces, has historically faced systemic marginalization. Kurdish demands for cultural and social autonomy have often been met with harsh repression, including military crackdowns and restrictions on the use of the Kurdish language in education and media. This approach has perpetuated grievances and led to cycles of resistance and retaliation (Yildiz and Breau 2021). The state's characterization of

18 By employing vague and ambiguously defined accusations the regime strategically manipulates public discourse to delegitimize dissent and normalize its authority. This tactic exemplifies ideological hegemony because it allows the state to present its actions as necessary and justified within a shared framework of national interest and moral order, even when those actions suppress alternative viewpoints or minority identities. The ambiguity of these accusations ensures that opposition can be broadly interpreted and punished, reinforcing the regime's dominance not only through legal and police powers but also through the internalization of its ideological narratives by the public.

Bahá'í International Community. (2008). *The Bahá'í Question: Cultural Cleansing in Iran*. New York: Bahá'í International Community. https://www.bic.org/sites/default/files/pdf/TheBahaiQuestion.pdf

Kurdish aspirations as a threat to national security, labeling them as separatist, has further marginalized this community, fostering a sense of "otherness" that challenges the country's territorial integrity.

Similarly, the Baluch people, concentrated in the southeastern province of Sistan and Baluchistan, suffer from severe economic underdevelopment and systemic neglect. Despite the region's strategic importance, it remains one of the poorest in Iran, marked by chronic deficiencies in education, healthcare, and infrastructure. Khan and Laoutides (2024) affirm that Baluchistan is a deeply underdeveloped region, where the population's lack of access to basic public services is exacerbated by entrenched political marginalization, further embedding the cycle of deprivation. The central government's securitization of the region, justified by concerns over drug trafficking and cross-border insurgencies, has led to widespread human rights violations, including extra-judicial killings and arbitrary detentions (Alam Saleh and Azizi 2022).

The Arab population in the oil-rich province of Khuzestan faces persistent systemic discrimination. Despite its significant contribution to Iran's economy through oil and gas resources, the province remains among the country's most underdeveloped, marked by high poverty and unemployment, conditions further exacerbated by the long-term impacts of the Iran–Iraq War. The region's Arab population, in particular, frequently reports systemic marginalization, including exclusion from political representation and cultural expression. As Daghagheleh (2023) highlights in Indigenous Refusal, the Iranian state has actively suppressed Arab identity through policies aimed at banning Arabic language and music and restricting the celebration of Arab cultural traditions, thereby deepening the community's political and cultural disenfranchisement. These grievances are not confined to cultural issues alone. As Samiee (2022) notes, they have manifested in ecological protests, particularly over water scarcity, reflecting a broader discontent with systemic neglect and environmental injustice endured by Khuzestan's Arab communities. The state's suppression of Arab protests and accusations of separatism further deepen the divide, fostering a sense of alienation and injustice (Hanieh 2020).

These communities are not only ethnically, culturally, and linguistically distinct but also religiously diverse, encompassing Sunni, Yarsan, Jafari, Christian, Bahá'í, and Jewish populations. This religious plurality further differentiates them from the Shiʿa-centric identity promoted by the central state, thereby intensifying their sociopolitical exclusion and subjection to repressive state policies. Within these communities, women experience a layered and compounded form of marginalization. Women from these minority groups are doubly burdened, subjected to state-enforced Islamic legal frameworks that restrict their autonomy, while simultaneously navigating patriarchal norms embedded within their local traditions. These conditions silence their voices within broader national and community discourses, where gendered governance and cultural homogenization function to erase subaltern subjectivities.

The cultural construction of ethnic "otherness" in Iran is reinforced through state narratives that portray some ethnic groups as politically disloyal or security threats. This discourse legitimizes centralized power and the repression of dissent under the guise of national unity, while homogenizing identity and marginalizing pluralism. However, these exclusionary policies have proven counterproductive; rather than fostering cohesion, they have deepened inter-ethnic distrust, catalyzed localized resistance movements, and exacerbated the very fragmentation the state seeks to contain. The result is a volatile landscape of contested belonging, where marginalized groups continue to resist both symbolic erasure and material dispossession (Elling and Saleh 2016).

The Repression of Political Dissent

The Islamic revolution, initially driven by a broad coalition of political forces such as leftists, secularists, nationalists, and Islamists, soon saw the rise of a theocratic regime that systematically targeted and silenced dissenting voices, particularly those that challenged the new political order (Keddie 2006). Political repression in post-revolutionary Iran has extended beyond opposition parties to include intellectuals, activists, and others critical of state policies, while also operating through processes of othering that construct dissenting individuals as outsiders or enemies to the political and moral order. Women have been particularly vulnerable, facing compounded forms of oppression shaped by both gender and political engagement.

Political parties that were initially part of the revolutionary struggle and were predominantly Muslim and Shia, such as the Tudeh Party,[19] the National Front,[20] and the Mojahedin-e Khalq,[21] quickly found themselves in direct conflict with the new Islamic government. The Tudeh Party, which had supported the overthrow of the Shah, was deemed a threat to the Islamic state and banned shortly after the revolution. Key members of the party, along with others from the National Front and Mojahedin-e Khalq, were arrested, tortured, and executed. Thousands were imprisoned, and many were executed without trial, including many young women and girls. The regime's violent purges continued throughout the 1980s, with political activists either forced into exile, imprisoned, or executed (Keddie 2006).

The suppression of political dissent, often accompanied by processes of othering, has extended across multiple sectors of society from the post-revolutionary period to the present, particularly targeting individuals in artistic, academic, and media communities perceived as potential challengers to state authority. Many

19 https://www.tudehpartyiran.org/en/home/, https://merip.org/1980/03/the-tudeh-party-in-iranian-politics/

20 https://www.britannica.com/topic/National-Front-Party

21 https://www.cfr.org/backgrounder/mujahadeen-e-khalq-mek, https://english.mojahedin.org/

renowned figures who had contributed to Iranian culture before the revolution were forced into silence or exile (Amnesty International 2020). Journalists and activists who attempted to report the truth about government policies or human rights abuses faced extreme repression under the Islamic Republic of Iran. Prominent activists such as Zhila Bani Yaghoub,[22] an Iranian journalist, writer, and human rights advocate, have been outspoken in championing women's rights, political freedom, and the protection of journalists in Iran. Narges Mohammadi,[23] a human rights lawyer and Nobel Peace Prize laureate in 2023, also faced severe repression for her efforts to promote women's rights after the revolution. More recently, journalists like Niloofar Hamedi (2022),[24] one of the first to report on the death of Mahsa Amini, have endured similar harassment, arrest, imprisonment, and censorship. The Iranian government has used these tools to stifle critical voices and prevent any challenge to its policies.[25]

The systematic targeting of journalists, activists, and intellectuals in Iran reflects the regime's use of ideological hegemony and processes of othering to suppress dissent. Through these mechanisms, critical voices are cast as outsiders, or even enemies, to the dominant political and moral order, legitimizing their exclusion and persecution. This repression underscores the regime's insistence on conformity to its political and religious narrative, where loyalty to the Supreme Leader or adherence to Shia Islam offers no immunity from persecution. Women, in particular, face the most severe repression, as they have consistently challenged the dominant ideological framework, being at the forefront of social justice and gender equality movements (Kar 2011).

The Cultural Construction of Otherness

Since the 1979 Islamic Revolution, the Iranian state has strategically employed media and formal education to construct a hegemonic national identity

22 She is known for her reporting on the social and political issues in Iran, particularly focusing on marginalized groups, including women and minorities. Bani Yaghoub was imprisoned multiple times due to her critical reporting, and she faced restrictions on her journalistic work. In addition, she has been banned from working as a journalist in Iran, illustrating the broader trend of repression and censorship faced by independent media figures in the country. Her case reflects the harsh treatment of women journalists who challenge the state's narrative and expose human rights abuses or criticize government policies. https://www.amnesty.org/en/latest/news/2012/09/iran-must-release-prisoner-of-conscience-zhila-bani-yaghoub/

23 https://www.nobelprize.org/prizes/peace/2023/mohammadi/facts/

24 https://www.uscirf.gov/religious-prisoners-conscience/forb-victims-database/niloofar-hamedi

25 Journalists critical of the government have been detained, tortured, and in some cases, executed. The state's censorship of the media has become an ongoing feature of the Islamic Republic's approach to controlling public opinion, creating a suffocating environment where freedom of expression is all but eradicated. Every public statement, article, or creative work has been scrutinized by the authorities, and those who dare speak out face consequences that include arrest, imprisonment, and even death (Amnesty International 2022).

rooted in Shi'a Islam, patriarchal norms, and revolutionary ideology. Central to this project is the production of otherness, whereby some ethnic, religious, gender-based, and ideological minorities are framed as deviant, threatening, or inferior. This process extends beyond symbolic representation, functioning as a practical instrument through which dissenting voices are constructed as outsiders, thereby justifying exclusion, suppressing opposition, and consolidating authoritarian control. Theoretical perspectives from Romero-Rodríguez et al. (2021) and Balibar (2006) illuminate how such constructions of otherness operate as socially produced and politically mobilized mechanisms that generate polarization and delineate the boundaries of belonging and citizenship. In this sense, otherness emerges not as an inherent condition but as a strategic tool of governance Building on this framework, this volume has identified four key processes through which state power enforces othering in Iranian society. The final category, in particular, highlights the cultural construction of difference as a central mechanism through which these exclusionary dynamics are normalized and sustained.

These theoretical insights on the cultural construction of Otherness are enacted in practice through state-controlled media, which actively disseminates narratives that both vilify marginalized groups and reinforce ideological conformity. Outlets such as Press TV and the Islamic Republic of Iran Broadcasting (IRIB) serve as central instruments in framing these groups as enemy or as agents of Western imperialism. As Saeidi and Vafa (2019) note, the post-revolutionary state utilizes these public platforms to construct and reinforce ideological boundaries that marginalize dissenting voices and elevate conformity to state ideology. Similarly, Golkar (2016) argues that the state's use of mass media functions to "paralyze" civil society through fear, misinformation, and the normalization of authoritarianism.

The formal and public educational system mirrors this ideological project too. From primary textbooks to university syllabi, curricula are designed to cultivate loyalty to the Islamic Republic while erasing or distorting alternative narratives. For example, religious and nationalist propaganda saturates history books, which portray pre-Islamic and non-Shi'a cultures as morally inferior or politically suspect (Nakhaei 2020). Courses on ethics and Islamic thought often implicitly (and sometimes explicitly) demonize secularism, feminism, and ethnic pluralism. As Khiabany (2009) highlights, this is part of a broader strategy where "modern" media tools are co-opted to reinforce a regressive ideological regime. Educational television programming and cultural productions reinforce dominant narratives by valorizing martyrdom, vilifying Western lifestyles, and constructing gender roles that legitimize the subordination of women. Varzi (2002) explores how wartime media and youth programming post-revolution have contributed to a militarized identity culture in which dissent is equated with treachery. This ideological rigidity breeds suspicion and hostility, not only between the state and society, but also among citizens, fostering a culture of mutual distrust.

State mechanisms, through tools such as media, education, art, and cultural productions, actively construct and reinforce cultural norms of otherness, thereby deepening sociopolitical cleavages and inhibiting the formation of democratic solidarity. As Golkar (2016) asserts, the "manipulated society" becomes incapable of mobilizing against injustice due to internalized narratives that delegitimize collective action. The concept of Otherness thus does not merely marginalize, it fragments society, entrenching long-standing patterns of inequality, alienation, and authoritarian control.

Conclusion

This chapter has demonstrated that the totalitarian logic of the post-1979 Islamic Republic is fundamentally sustained through the construction and enforcement of a singular, hegemonic national identity, one that systematically marginalizes all who fall outside its narrowly defined religious, gendered, ethnic, and ideological boundaries. The Bahá'í community illustrates this process with particular clarity: across state media, educational curricula, and public discourse, Bahá'ís are depicted as deviant or subversive, a discursive strategy that legitimizes their exclusion from the national body. This dynamic, explored further in subsequent chapters, reveals how the regime weaponizes representation to police the limits of citizenship and belonging.

Building on this analysis, I have argued that the state's portrayal of minority religious, ethnic, and ideological groups as existential threats to Islam and the Islamic state produces a dichotomous political imaginary grounded in an antagonistic "us versus them" logic. This practice echoes postcolonial and decolonial critiques (Said 1978; Mignolo 2011), which interpret such strategies as forms of internal colonization aimed at erasing plurality and imposing cultural homogeneity in service of centralized power. The five interlocking modalities of otherness identified in this chapter function as an integrated system of structural exclusion, maintained not only through coercive state apparatuses but also through pervasive discursive and ideological mechanisms. Drawing on Hannah Arendt (1951) and Antonio Gramsci (1971), the chapter shows how the regime normalizes exclusionary narratives that render hierarchy and domination both intelligible and necessary. In doing so, it restricts the horizon of collective political imagination, deepens social fragmentation, forecloses inclusive citizenship, and curtails the emergence of a democratic public sphere.

Within this broader framework of state-produced otherness and ideological homogenization, the experiences of marginalized groups, particularly women from religious minorities, reveal how structural oppression intersects with gender and modes of resistance. These dynamics not only illuminate the lived realities of those pushed to the margins but also set the conceptual foundation for the following chapters, which examine the agency, resilience, and transformative activism of Bahá'í women in the context of the WLF movement.

Bibliography

AI-assisted tools, including Grammarly, were used for language editing and structural clarity. The author retained full responsibility for the intellectual content of the chapter.

Afary, Janet. 2009. *Sexual Politics in Modern Iran.* Cambridge: Cambridge University Press.

Aghajanian, Alireza, and Amir Merat. 2020. *Ethnicity and State Building in Modern Iran.* Cambridge: Cambridge University Press.

Ahmed, Sara. 2000. *Strange Encounters: Embodied Others in Post-Coloniality.* Routledge.

Alam Saleh, A., and M. Azizi. 2022. "Securitization and Ethnic Minorities in Iran: A Baluch Perspective." *Middle Eastern Studies* 58 (3): 1–15.

Amnesty International. 2020. *Iran: Trampling Humanity: Mass Arrests, Disappearances and Torture Since Iran's November 2019 Protests*. Index No. MDE 13/2891/2020. London: Amnesty International. https://www.amnesty.org/en/documents/mde13/2891/2020/en.

Amnesty International. 2022. *Iran: Human Rights Groups Sound Alarm Against Draconian Internet Bill.* March 17, 2022. Amnesty International. https://www.amnesty.org/en/documents/mde13/5361/2022/en/.

Arat, Yeşim. 1994. "Toward a Democratic Society: The Women's Movement in Turkey in the 1980s." *Women's Studies International Forum* 17 (2–3): 241–248.

Arendt, Hannah. 1951. *The Origins of Totalitarianism*. New York: Harcourt, Brace.

Azimi, Fakhreddin. 2006. *Intellectuals and the Islamic Revolution*. London: I.B. Tauris.

Badran, Margot. 2009. *Feminism in the Middle East: A History of Struggle and Transformation*. Princeton: Princeton University Press.

Bahá'í International Community. 2023. *The Bahá'í Question: Persecution and Resilience in Iran*. https://www.bic.org/sites/default/files/pdf/tbq_2023_f_screen.pdf

Balibar, Étienne. 2006. *Strangers as Enemies: Further Reflections on the Aporias of Transnational Citizenship*. Globalization Working Paper 06/4. Hamilton, ON: Institute on Globalization and the Human Condition, McMaster University.

Bayat, Asef. 2013. *Life as Politics: How Ordinary People Change the Middle East*. 2nd ed. Stanford, CA: Stanford University Press. ISBN 9780804783262.

Bhabha, Homi K. 2004. *The Location of Culture*. 2nd ed. Routledge.

Charrad, Mounira M. 2001. *States and Women's Rights: The Making of Postcolonial Tunisia, Algeria, and Morocco*. Berkeley: University of California Press.

Chehabi, Houchang E. 1991. "Religion and Politics in Iran: How Theocratic Is the Islamic Republic?" *Daedalus* 120 (3): 69–91.

Cockroft, James. 1979. "Iran's Khomeini." *Seven Days* 3 (February 23): 19–20.

Dadpour, Rana. 2025, August 18. "Theocratic Authoritarian Urbanism and Performative Right to the City: A Case Study of Tehran's City Theatre." *City*. https://doi.org/10.1080/13604813.2025.2541461, https://www.tandfonline.com/doi/pdf/10.1080/13604813.2025.2541461

Daghagheleh, Aghil. 2023. *Indigenous Refusal: Arab Minority and the Formation of Modern State in Iran*. PhD diss., Rutgers, The State University of New Jersey.

Elling, Rasmus Christian, and A. Saleh. 2016. "Ethnic Minorities and the Politics of Identity in Iran." *Iranian Studies* 49 (1): 159–171. https://doi.org/10.1080/00210862.2016.1118949.

Foucault, Michel. 1978. *The History of Sexuality, Volume 1: An Introduction*. Translated by Robert Hurley. New York: Pantheon Books.

Göle, Nilüfer. 2011. "The Civilizational, Spatial, and Sexual Powers of the Secular." In *Varieties of Secularism in a Secular Age*, edited by Michael Warner, Jonathan Van Antwerpen, and Craig Calhoun, 243–264. Cambridge, MA: Harvard University Press.

Golkar, Saeid. 2016, June. "Manipulated Society: Paralyzing the Masses in Post-Revolutionary Iran." *International Journal of Politics, Culture, and Society* 29 (2): 139–161. https://doi.org/10.1007/s10767-015-9208-0.

Gramsci, Antonio. 1971. *Selections from the Prison Notebooks*. Edited and translated by Quintin Hoare and Geoffrey Nowell Smith. New York: International Publishers.

Hamedi, Niloofar. 2022. *Iranian Journalists in the Age of Censorship: Personal Accounts*. International Press Institute.

Hanieh, Adam. 2020. "Khuzestan and the Politics of Marginalization in Iran." *Journal of Middle Eastern Affairs* 12 (4): 45–67.

Iran Human Rights Documentation Center. 2022. *State of Coercion: The Situation of Sunni Muslims in Iran*. New Haven, CT: Iran Human Rights Documentation Center.

Kar, Mehrangiz. 2011. *Women's Rights in Iran: A Historical Perspective*. Oxford: Oxford University Press.

Keddie, Nikki. 2006. *The Iranian Revolution: Its Impact on the Middle East and Beyond*. Princeton: Princeton University Press.

Khan, Seema, and Costas Laoutides. 2024. "Trapped between Religion and Ethnicity: Identity Politics against the Baloch in Iran and Pakistan." *Dynamics of Asymmetric Conflict* 17 (2): 164–184. https://doi.org/10.1080/17467586.2024.2356508.

Khiabany, Gholam. 2009. *Iranian Media: The Paradox of Modernity*. 1st ed. London: Routledge. https://doi.org/10.4324/9780203876411.

Levinas, Emmanuel. 1969. *Totality and Infinity: An Essay on Exteriority*. Translated by Alphonso Lingis. Pittsburgh: Duquesne University Press.

Mahdavi, Pardis. 2017. "The Politics of Gender in Contemporary Iran." *Women's Studies International Forum* 60: 34–42.

Mahmood, Saba. 2005. *Politics of Piety: The Islamic Revival and the Feminist Subject*. Princeton, NJ: Princeton University Press.

Mahmood, Saba. 2016. *Religious Difference in a Secular Age: A Minority Report*. Princeton University Press.

Martin, D. 1979. *The Persecution of the Bahá'ís in Iran. Seven Days, 31.* (Interview from December 1978, published in the February 23, 1979, issue of Seven Days).

Mbembe, Achille. 2003. "Necropolitics." *Public Culture* 15 (1): 11–40. https://mirror.explodie.org/Public%20Culture-2003-Mbembe-11-40.pdf

Mignolo, Walter D. 2011. *The Darker Side of Western Modernity: Global Futures, Decolonial Options*. Durham, NC: Duke University Press.

Moghadam, Valentine M. 2003. *Modernizing Women: Gender and Social Change in the Middle East*. Boulder: Lynne Rienner.

Mohammadpour, Ahmad, and Kamal Soleimani. 2021. "'Minoritisation' of the Other: The Iranian Ethno-Theocratic State's Assimilatory Strategies." *Postcolonial Studies* 24 (1): 40–62. https://doi.org/10.1080/13688790.2020.1746157.

Mojab, Shahrzad. 2001. "The Politics of Women's Rights in Iran: Gender, Political Participation, and Social Change." *Women's Studies International Forum* 24 (6): 657–667.

Nakhaei, Nima. 2020. *State and Development in Post-Revolutionary Iran*. PhD diss., York University. https://yorkspace.library.yorku.ca/handle/10315/37610.

Romero-Rodríguez, Luis M., Sabina Civila, and Ignacio Aguaded. 2021. "Otherness as a Form of Intersubjective Social Exclusion: Conceptual Discussion from the Current Communicative Scenario." *Journal of Information, Communication and Ethics in Society* 19 (1): 20–37. https://doi.org/10.1108/JICES-11-2019-0130.

Sabet Sarvestany, Raha. 2023. *Civil Resistance and the Hijab and Chastity Bill*. Accessed April 25, 2025. https://www.hra-news.org/articles/a-1128/.

Sabet Sarvestany, Raha. 2025. *Executions in the Islamic Republic: Symbolic Violence and the Reproduction of Power*. Accessed April 25, 2025. https://www.peace-mark.org/articles/168-7/.

Saeidi, Shirin, and Aylin Vafa. 2019. "After Isolation: Mirrors between Parallel Worlds and New Conceptual Spaces of Activism in Post-Revolutionary Iran." *Millennium* 47 (3): 417–443. https://doi.org/10.1177/0305829819840800

Said, Edward W. 1978. *Orientalism*. New York: Pantheon Books.

Sajoo, Amyn B. 2014. "Minority Rights in the Middle East." *Ethics & Global Politics* 7 (1). https://doi.org/10.3402/egp.v7.23351, https://www.researchgate.net/publication/307649482_Minority_Rights_in_the_Middle_East

Samiee, Maziar. 2022. "Beyond Rentier State and Climate: Clashing Environmental Imaginaries and Ecological Oppression in Iran." In *Enforcing Ecocide: Power, Policing & Planetary Militarization*, edited by Alexander Dunlap, Andrea Brock, and Maziar Samiee, [page range]. [Publisher].

Sanasarian, Eliz. 2000. *Religious Minorities in Iran*. Cambridge University Press. https://assets.cambridge.org/97805217/70736/frontmatter/9780521770736_frontmatter.pdf

United Nations Office of the High Commissioner for Human Rights. 2024. "Iran: Experts Alarmed at Systematic Targeting of Bahá'í Women." December 23, 2024. *OHCHR*. https://www.ohchr.org/en/press-releases/2024/12/iran-experts-alarmed-systematic-targeting-bahai-women.

Varzi, Roxanne. 2002. *Visionary Terrains of Post-Revolution Iran: War, Youth Culture, Media and Public Space*. PhD diss., Columbia University. ProQuest Dissertations & Theses Global (3066918).

Yeganeh, Roya. 2001. "Women's Legal Rights in Iran: A Historical and Legal Perspective." *Middle Eastern Studies* 37 (2): 32–45.

Yildiz, Kerim, and Susan Breau. 2021. *The Kurds: Culture and Identity in Contemporary Middle East*. London: Palgrave Macmillan.

Zabihi-Moghaddam, S. 2016. "State-Sponsored Persecution of Baha'is in the Islamic Republic of Iran." *Contemporary Review of the Middle East* 3 (2): 124–146.

Zaynab, Sara. 2015. *Gender, Society, and Religion in Iran: Exploring Cultural and Social Narratives*. London: Routledge.

1 Research Methodology and Theoretical Foundations

Introduction

Central to this study is the concept of faith-based agency, which I conceptualize as a non-oppositional form of epistemic and moral action grounded not in reactive resistance to the state but in the generative ethical obligations of religious commitment. From this perspective, spirituality extends beyond private belief or abstract mysticism to encompass a process of capacity-building that cultivates individual intellectual development alongside a lived ethical orientation toward community-building. Rooted in Bahá'í teachings on justice, unity, and service to humanity, this form of agency reflects an evolving maturity of human capacity (Shoghi Effendi, *World Order*, 163–165).

This conception of agency aligns with Saba Mahmood's (2005) theory of *ethical agency*, which critiques secular notions of autonomy by demonstrating how religious disciplines can cultivate moral clarity and meaningful social action. In this context, *spiritual identity* – a sense of self rooted in religious beliefs and practices, encompassing one's understanding of life's purpose, moral obligations, and belonging in relation to a higher truth or divine order – forms the foundation of ethical subjectivity. This mode of being, shaped by internalized ethical frameworks (Mahmood 2005), guides individuals in responding to power, suffering, and injustice, enabling women, particularly minority and marginalized, to interpret adversity, resist oppression, and sustain hope through actions informed by theological ethics and communal responsibility.

Methodologically, this study employs a qualitative and interdisciplinary approach that draws on life-narrative and discourse analysis, and archival research. By integrating both insider and outsider perspectives, it seeks to engage ethically and rigorously with the lived experiences of Bahá'í women in post-revolutionary Iran. Drawing on oral testimonies, social media discourse, and historical documentation, the research foregrounds the intersection of faith-based agency, collective identity, and intersubjective resilience in the face of systemic persecution. At the heart of this framework lies a carefully curated corpus of 20 narratives documenting the persecution of Bahá'ís in Iran. The selection of these life narratives arises not only from scholarly

DOI: 10.4324/9781003567370-2

concerns but also from deep personal motivations, reflecting my own connection to the lives and struggles they illuminate. This position shapes the research process itself, ensuring that the narratives are engaged not merely as texts to be analyzed but as testimonies to which I remain personally and ethically accountable.

As a researcher closely engaged with these lived experiences, I approach this work with sustained reflexive awareness of my positionality. Following Chiseri-Strater's (1996) emphasis on reflexivity, I acknowledge that my identity, values, and personal history shape the narratives selected, the questions posed, and the interpretations developed. My connection to the Bahá'í community, through shared faith, cultural familiarity, and personal relationships, at times situates me as an insider, affording access to intimate experiences and affective dimensions of these narratives. At the same time, as Mohammad (2001) suggests, positionality is fluid and relational; I also occupy outsider positions within academic and institutional contexts, where questions of representation, authority, and power must be critically negotiated. This dual positioning necessitates an ongoing reflexive praxis that remains critically attentive to the ethical complexities of knowledge production concerning a systematically persecuted community.

A central component of this study engages with the testimonies of ten Bahá'í women and young girls executed in a single night in Shiraz, my hometown. Among them was my second cousin, Akhtar Sabet Sarvestany, whose story, along with those of the others, had a profound impact on my upbringing and personal understanding of faith, persecution, agency, and resilience. These narratives constitute both the emotional and analytical core of this research and are closely intertwined with my own experiences of imprisonment. Additional cases are selected based on their historical and analytical significance. For instance, Chapter 1 focuses on the contemporary experiences of Mahvash Sabet and Fariba Kamal Abadi, whose prolonged imprisonment, spanning over thirteen years, provides critical insight into ongoing forms of faith-based agency and resilience, particularly in the context of the WLF movement in 2022.

The methodological approach in Chapter 1 combines insider and outsider perspectives through two primary sources: a published interview I conducted with Mahvash Sabet[1] and a discourse analysis of social media activity produced by close family members, particularly their children and relatives. These digital narratives, shared on platforms such as Twitter and Instagram, document prison visits, emotional responses, and evolving forms of solidarity. While the interview provides firsthand testimony of systemic exclusion and the psychological dimensions of persecution, the analysis of social media discourse offers an external yet intimate perspective on relational resilience and

1 https://elixir-journal.org/issue13/interview2.php

networks of care. Together, these sources illuminate both the mechanisms of state violence and the emergent, relational forms of resistance that transcend ideological and religious boundaries.

Chapter 4 adopts a primarily chronological organization, beginning with the life of Ṭáhirih, a seminal figure in Bahá'í history and an early advocate of gender equality. Subsequent narratives are selected based on patterns of loss, endurance, and relational suffering, particularly among women who experienced the execution or imprisonment of close family members. This selection enables a nuanced analysis of how agency and resilience are enacted by members of religious minority communities under conditions of extreme repression. The research further draws on a range of archival and secondary sources. These include *Love at the Cost of Life* (Rahimi 2011), a collection of testimonies by Bahá'í women in exile,[2] and over 500 video-recorded interviews conducted by Shapour Daneshmand for the documentary project *A Quiet Genocide*.[3] Although the documentary remains unreleased, these interviews constitute a significant and underutilized archive of memory and resistance.

Additional materials are drawn from the *Archives of Bahá'í Persecution in Iran*, curated by the Bahá'í International Community,[4] and *The Bahá'í World*, a series of volumes published by the Universal House of Justice documenting global Bahá'í contributions and experiences. The most recent volume (Vol. 35, 2025)[5] provides valuable contemporary insights into the community's response to ongoing repression. Thus, methodologically, this study combines life narrative analysis with intersectional feminist frameworks, while also attending to the affective dimensions of memory, trauma, and testimony. The aim is not only to document these experiences but to analyze them as dynamic sites of ethical subjectivity, faith-based agency, and collective resistance.

By situating Bahá'í women's lived experiences within intersectional and feminist frameworks, this chapter reconceptualizes spirituality as a form of embodied, relational agency across three thematic strands: intersectionality in the context of Bahá'í Women in Iran, Bahá'í women's negotiation of agency

2 "Love at the Cost of Life" is a historical account of Bahá'í women forced to flee Iran after the Islamic Revolution. The author, Pooran Rahimi, an Iranian Bahá'í herself, left the country after her family faced threats of arrest and property confiscation. In her book, she conducted open, informal interviews with selected Bahá'í women, allowing them to share their life stories, from joyful moments to their eventual exile.

3 see: https://vimeo.com/54648076

Daneshmand (2010), a non-Bahá'í Iranian who left Iran before the Islamic Revolution, founded a project to document and publicize the persecution of Bahá'ís in Iran through media. His initiative, *A Quiet Genocide*, includes over 500 videotaped interviews. Drawing on his documentation skills, Daneshmand presents the Bahá'í experience from an outsider's perspective, aiming to better understand the faith and its community through personal narratives. When he interviewed me in 2015, his analytical approach showed a genuine effort to grasp the depth of Bahá'í oppression.

4 https://iranBahá'ípersecution.bic.org/node

5 https://news.bahai.org/story/1774/

within constraining structures, and the significance of Bahá'í identity in sustaining resilience. Together, these discussions offer a counterpoint to narratives that equate agency solely with overt opposition, demonstrating instead that spiritually motivated action and purposeful ethical practice constitute powerful, if often recognized, modes of resistance (Mahmood 2005; Scott 1990). In doing so, the chapter contributes to decolonizing dominant theories of agency and resistance by foregrounding the transformative potential of spiritual subjectivities under conditions of constraint.

Intersectionality in the Context of Bahá'í Women in Iran

The concept of intersectionality, introduced by Kimberlé Crenshaw (1989), provides a critical framework for analyzing how overlapping axes of identity, such as race, gender, class, and religion, produce compounded forms of oppression. Moving beyond single-axis approaches, it highlights how marginalization emerges through the interaction of multiple structures of power. Subsequent scholarship has extended this framework across diverse contexts, including migration (Anthias 2012), religious discrimination (Bilge 2013), disability studies (Erevelles and Minear 2010), and postcolonial feminism (Mohanty 2003), enabling more nuanced analyses of systemic inequality.

Applied to the case of Bahá'í women in Iran, intersectionality reveals how religious, gendered, legal, and sociopolitical forces converge to produce layered forms of exclusion. Within the ideological and legal framework of the Islamic Republic, discrimination is institutionalized through policies that simultaneously target religious minorities and women. As members of the largest unrecognized non-Muslim minority, Bahá'ís face state-sanctioned persecution, including restricted access to education, employment discrimination, and denial of civil rights, while women are further constrained by patriarchal legal structures. Bahá'í women thus occupy a particularly vulnerable position at the intersection of these systems of domination. Their experiences underscore the need for an intersectional lens that captures the mutually reinforcing dynamics of religious persecution and gender inequality, while also revealing the ethical and spiritual frameworks through which they navigate and contest these conditions.

From a Bahá'í Perspective, gender equality is not merely a spiritual principle but a fundamental social principle essential for the advancement of humanity. 'Abdu'l-Bahá[6] articulates this vision by stating, "The world of hu-

6 'Abdu'l-Bahá (23 May 1844–28 November 1921), the eldest son of Bahá'u'lláh, was appointed as his successor and led the Bahá'í Faith from 1892 until his death. Born into an aristocratic family in Tehran, his early life was marked by hardship after his father's imprisonment and their subsequent exile. The family lived in Baghdad, Istanbul, and Edirne before being confined in the prison city of 'Akká (Acre), where 'Abdu'l-Bahá remained until his release in 1908 at age 64.

manity has two wings, one is women and the other men. Not until both wings are equally developed can the bird fly. Should one wing remain weak, flight is impossible" ('Abdu'l-Bahá 1982, 318). This imagery underscores the necessity of gender equality for both intellectual and societal progress, emphasizing that the full development of civilization depends on the equal participation of women and men. Within this framework, disparities in capacity or achievement are not viewed as justification for inequality but as conditions requiring redress through equitable access to education and opportunity. According to 'Abdu'l-Bahá, "The only remedy is education, opportunity; for equality means equal qualification" ('Abdu'l-Bahá 1982, 76).

Education, therefore, occupies a central role in the Bahá'í conceptualization and practice of gender equality. 'Abdu'l-Bahá emphasizes that "the principle of religion has been revealed by Bahá'u'lláh that woman must be given the privilege of equal education with man and full right to his prerogatives" ('Abdu'l-Bahá 1982, 108). He argues that eliminating educational disparities will enable women to achieve equal capacity and significance within the social and economic domains, ultimately fostering global harmony. He further contends that humanity's historical inefficiency and conflict stem from the exclusion of women from key societal roles. The education of women, he asserts, "will be a mighty step toward [war's] abolition and ending, for she will use her whole influence against war" ('Abdu'l-Bahá 1982, 108). Women's role in shaping the next generation through child-rearing and moral education is framed as a decisive force in promoting peace and ending warfare, as women are positioned as natural advocates for nonviolence and international cooperation.

Beyond education, Bahá'í perspective highlights the importance of women's participation in industrial and agricultural sciences, emphasizing that "by this means she will demonstrate capability and ensure recognition of equality in the social and economic equation" ('Abdu'l-Bahá 1982, 283). Moreover, he attributes to women "greater moral courage than the man" and unique capacities for leadership, particularly in moments of crisis ('Abdu'l-Bahá 1982, 103). These perspectives articulate a theological and social foundation for gender equality within the Bahá'í Faith, framing women's empowerment as integral not only to individual development but also to the broader advancement of society. Consequently, the Bahá'í understanding of gender equality offers a distinctive lens through which Bahá'í women interpret their agency and educational rights, one that aligns with, yet also departs from, dominant feminist theories and ideologies. While it resonates with broader feminist discourses on education, agency, and structural equality, it remains grounded in

---

'Abdu'l-Bahá devoted himself to advancing his father's Faith, establishing Bahá'í institutions, and promoting peace, unity, and social progress. After his release, traveled to Egypt, Europe, and North America playing a crucial role in spreading Bahá'í teachings worldwide.

a spiritual and moral worldview that positions gender equality as essential to achieving global peace and fostering societal progress.

Since the Islamic Revolution of 1979, the Bahá'ís of Iran have continued to devote sustained effort to articulating, embodying, and socializing the foundational principles of their Faith, despite operating under conditions of intensified repression. Prior to and after the Revolution, the Iranian Bahá'í community played an active role in education, capacity-building, and socio-economic development, alongside meaningful contributions to cultural and artistic life. These long-standing endeavors reflect a holistic vision of human progress that seeks to harmonize spiritual conviction with material advancement. Within this context, the agency of Bahá'í women and their communities becomes particularly visible. Their continued engagement in educational initiatives, grassroots development projects, and ethical forms of civic participation demonstrates a sustained commitment to collective upliftment across cities in Iran, as illustrated throughout the various chapters. I conceptualize this phenomenon as *Societal Contributions and Visibility* (SC and V), a form of faith-based civic agency characterized by resilience, moral clarity, and sustained public service. These actions are not simply adaptive responses to marginalization; rather, they represent intentional interventions in the social sphere that challenge reductive narratives portraying religious minorities solely as passive victims.

Yet under the post-revolutionary state, this growing visibility has often heightened the vulnerability of Bahá'ís. Their contributions, instead of being recognized as forms of national investment and social responsibility, are frequently interpreted by the state as challenges to its ideological authority. This paradox reveals a critical dynamic: the ethical, developmental, and community-building efforts of Bahá'í individuals specially women not only affirm their belonging and aspirations for Iran's future but simultaneously expose them to punitive forms of exclusion and repression. Thus, the marginalization of Bahá'í women in post-revolution Iran cannot be understood purely through the lens of religious or gender-based discrimination. A more comprehensive, intersectional analysis must consider their sociocultural contributions and the state's reaction to their faith-based agency, resilience, and visibility. This broader framing highlights how acts of service, rather than shielding them, become entangled with political vulnerability under authoritarian conditions.[7]

7 Many of these women navigate their marginalization by establishing informal networks of education for children in different subjects, supporting underground Bahá'í institutions such as BIHE, and participating in global advocacy efforts such as sharing their narratives, poems, photos, and reports of personal discriminations. Their resistance is not always overt but is embedded in everyday acts of survival, continuing to educate new generation despite state-imposed barriers, creating community support systems, and sustaining cultural and religious identity in the face of erasure.

Bahá'í Women Navigate and Negotiate Their Agency Within Constrained Structures

The concept of agency within structural constraints has been extensively explored in social theories, particularly in the works of Giddens (1984) and Bourdieu (1990). Giddens' theory of structuration posits that individuals, while operating within preexisting social structures, simultaneously shape and transform these structures through their actions. Bourdieu's notion of habitus similarly emphasizes how individuals internalize social constraints yet navigate and challenge them in ways that either reinforce or alter societal norms. In the context of marginalized communities, agency does not necessarily manifest as overt resistance; rather, it often takes the form of indirect, everyday acts of negotiation and resilience (Scott 1985).

Feminist scholars have further expanded on these theories, emphasizing the complexity of women's agency within systems of power. Butler (1997) challenges the binary of subordination and resistance, arguing that agency emerges through performativity, where individuals negotiate identity and power through repeated acts. Mahmood (2005) critiques Western liberal notions of agency as inherently linked to resistance, proposing instead that women's agency can manifest through engagement with, rather than opposition to, social and religious norms. Similarly, Mohanty (2003) highlights how women in marginalized communities exercise agency in ways that may not align with dominant feminist paradigms but remain significant acts of self-determination.

Building on these perspectives, scholars examining women's agency from a religious standpoint argue that agency is not necessarily tied to secular or oppositional forms of resistance but can be embedded within religious practices and frameworks. Mahmood (2005), Wadud (2006), and Barlas (2002) argue that religious interpretation and spiritual commitment can serve as sites for women's empowerment, enabling them to challenge patriarchal structures from within rather than rejecting them outright. Ali (2016) further explores how Muslim women assert agency through ethical and interpretive engagements with religious texts, demonstrating that agency within religious traditions is multifaceted and dynamic. These perspectives broaden the understanding of women's agency, illustrating that it can be exercised through various modes of engagement, adaptation, and transformation within secular and religious spheres.

In the case of Bahá'í women in Iran, agency is enacted within a deeply restrictive sociopolitical framework, constituted through the intersection of gendered subordination and state-sanctioned religious persecution. In addition to legal and institutional barriers that curtail their rights in both public and private spheres, these women face governmental resistance to their SC and V. As the narratives, accounts, and lived experiences of Bahá'í women in Iran demonstrate, agency persists despite these intersecting layers of oppression, emerging through practices of resilience and adaptation that are deeply rooted in the Bahá'í approach to social change.

At the heart of this approach lies a core Bahá'í teaching: that human nature encompasses both spiritual and material dimensions, which operate in dynamic interplay to shape personal conduct and societal transformation. This dual orientation informs the Bahá'í community's commitment to constructive engagement and moral resilience, even in the face of persistent marginalization. As Shoghi Effendi[8] articulates, "We cannot segregate the human heart from the environment outside us . . . Man is organic with the world. His inner life moulds the environment and is itself also deeply affected by it" (Shoghi Effendi 1993). This interdependence underscores the idea that meaningful and lasting social change necessitates both material progress and the moral transformation of individuals, including both the oppressed and those who sustain oppressive structures.

Rather than engaging in adversarial activism or partisan political opposition, the Bahá'í approach to social change foregrounds unity, constructive agency, and forms of service-oriented social action that seek to transform society through cooperation rather than confrontation. As the Universal House of Justice[9] asserts, "The working of the material world is merely a reflection of spiritual conditions, and until the spiritual conditions can be changed there can be no lasting change for the better in material affairs" (Universal House of Justice 1963–1986, 283). This principle informs the Bahá'í community's refusal to participate in political confrontation, emphasizing ethical engagement, education, and community-building as pathways to sustainable social transformation.

In light of the preceding discussion, Bahá'í women in Iran embody a distinctive form of agency characterized by constructive action, resilience, and a principled rejection of adversarial or divisive political engagement. Rooted in the Bahá'í vision of social transformation, this mode of agency prioritizes unity, nonviolence, and constructive participation in society rather than confrontation. At its core lies a commitment to selfless service and the promotion of collective well-being, values extended to all members of society, regardless of background or belief. Even under the most repressive conditions, this ethic of care and contribution remains a defining expression of their faith-based agency.

One of the most notable manifestations of this constructive resilience (Karlberg 2010) is the pursuit of higher education through alternative

8 He served as the Guardian of the Bahá'í Faith from 1922 until his passing in 1957. As the grandson and designated successor of 'Abdu'l-Bahá, he was entrusted with guiding the faith's development, overseeing the establishment of its global administrative structure, and directing a series of teaching plans that facilitated the expansion of the religion into new regions worldwide.

9 The Universal House of Justice, located at the Bahá'í World Centre in Haifa, has served as the supreme governing body of the Bahá'í Faith since its establishment in 1963. The institution was ordained by Bahá'u'lláh in the Kitáb-i-Aqdas, His most sacred book, revealed in 1873 in 'Akká.

structures such as the BIHE and the organization of moral and character development classes for children and junior youth.[10] Many Bahá'í women, alongside their male counterparts, have played a central role in advancing these educational initiatives. They serve as teachers, mentors, curriculum developers, and administrators, ensuring the continued transmission of knowledge and the preservation of their community's intellectual and cultural capital dynamic illustrated in Mahvash Sabet's testimony in Chapter 1.

Beyond their participation in informal educational structures, numerous Bahá'í women have transformed their homes into informal learning spaces where children, students, and educators can gather, exchange resources, and continue their studies under restrictive conditions. Others contribute materially by providing meals, shelter, or logistical support, further reinforcing a communal ethic of care and solidarity. These actions exemplify not only resilience in the face of systemic oppression but also a profound commitment to gender equality, community upliftment, and the continuity of educational and cultural life under legal and societal constraints.

In addition to their educational engagement, Bahá'í women frequently pursue entrepreneurial activities as a response to economic marginalization. When state authorities close the businesses or terminate the employment of Bahá'í breadwinners, women often step in by launching small enterprises. These may include producing artisanal goods, managing home-based food services and operating private hair salons in their houses, or offering community training in fields such as art, fitness, and handicrafts.[11] Such efforts not only secure livelihoods but also promote social integration by fostering economic ties with broader Iranian society. Through these educational, entrepreneurial, and communal engagements, Bahá'í women embody a form of faith-based and epistemological agency that challenges social exclusion, sustains communal life, and reclaims spaces of dignity and participation under repression.

Beyond their contributions to education and economic sustainability, Bahá'í women play a vital role in providing psychosocial and emotional support to individuals and families affected by state violence, including imprisonment, torture, and execution. Since the 1979 Islamic Revolution, over 200 Bahá'ís have been executed, tortured to death, or forcibly disappeared, and thousands more have faced arrest, interrogation, or imprisonment. Bahá'í women, alongside men, have themselves been subjected to imprisonment and

10 https://www.bahai.org/action/family-life-children/childrens-classes, https://bahaiteachings.org/bahai-core-activities/

11 These data were collected through systematic observation of publicly accessible Instagram accounts of Iranian Bahá'í women who advertise and offer professional services. The analysis reveals that some of these women extend their services beyond Iran, utilizing digital platforms to provide online work and engage transnationally.

torture, yet those who remain outside prison walls have assumed crucial roles in sustaining affected families and communities.

Their resilience manifests not only in personal endurance but also in acts of solidarity and care. Women often assume caregiving responsibilities for children whose parents are incarcerated,[12] while others organize informal networks of support to assist families during times of crisis. A striking example of this communal ethic is the presence of Bahá'í women at prison gates, where they offer warm tea in winter or cold water in summer to families visiting their loved ones. I personally encountered this practice during a visit to Rajaee Shahr Prison,[13] where such simple acts, sharing a drink or a word of comfort, offered more than physical relief. They created a space for storytelling, empathy, and mutual recognition among families bearing similar grief.

In the broader context of how minority women negotiate their agency within constraining structures, the everyday actions of Bahá'í women in Iran exemplify a distinctive form of nonviolent agency known as constructive resilience, a faith-based praxis grounded in service, empathy, and social harmony. These modest yet intentional practices reflect a theological commitment to the oneness of humanity, positioning compassion and solidarity as meaningful expressions of epistemic agency. Within the authoritarian context of the Islamic Republic, such acts function not only as strategies of survival but also as quiet counter-hegemonic interventions that unsettle the isolating and dehumanizing dynamics of state repression. Their service-oriented ethos, extending to both Bahá'ís and non-Bahá'ís, embodies a form of agency that is constitutive rather than reactive. Resonating with Saba Mahmood's (2005) conception of ethical subjectivity, this agency emerges through embodied moral discipline rather than overt political confrontation, reframing resilience as an active ethical engagement with one's social environment.

The practices of Bahá'í women demonstrate that agency is neither a fixed capacity exercised in opposition to structure nor entirely determined by external constraints. Instead, it is a negotiated process shaped by spiritual commitments, communal responsibilities, and the sociopolitical pressures of an authoritarian state. Through informal education networks, acts of care, and community-building efforts, they reconfigure socially coded roles to generate change from within. This mode of action aligns with Foucault's (1991) notion

12 Care is provided not only by close relatives, such as grandparents, but also by younger families who assume responsibility for children whose parents are imprisoned.

13 Rajaee Shahr Prison has long been associated with systematic human rights violations since the 1979 Islamic Revolution, including severe physical and psychological torture of political prisoners and prisoners of conscience, as well as executions carried out without due process. In the aftermath of the November 2019 protests, numerous detainees, including minors, were reportedly subjected to severe mistreatment within the prison. Credible accounts document instances of torture and other forms of cruel, inhuman, or degrading treatment, underscoring the persistence of coercive practices within the Iranian penal system. https://eur-lex.europa.eu/

of counter-conduct, a form of resistance enacted within dominant structures by mobilizing nonviolence, collective memory, and spiritual duty. In doing so, Bahá'í women articulate alternative epistemologies of resistance that challenge the universality of secular-liberal models of agency and offer a theologically informed, decolonial account of subjectivity and social transformation. Their consistent, quiet acts, rather than overt confrontation, preserve dignity, sustain community, and cultivate hope. Ultimately, their constructive resilience enriches contemporary feminist and political theory by illustrating how marginalized actors generate power through spiritual coherence and ethical steadfastness under conditions of repression.

The Significance of Bahá'í Identity in Sustaining Resilience

A key conceptual dimension of the Bahá'í community's resilience in Iran is that it extends beyond individual perseverance, functioning as a collective, historically embedded practice. Based on the life experiences and testimony documented in the archives on the persecution of Bahá'ís in Iran, this resilience emerges not as an isolated personal response but as a shared, intergenerational ethic of endurance, care, and principled action cultivated within the community over decades. This form of resilience is anchored in a shared social identity and reinforced through strong communal cohesion and adaptive strategies developed across nearly two centuries of sustained persecution. Social identity theory (Tajfel and Turner 1979) offers a powerful analytical framework for examining how Bahá'ís actively construct and maintain their collective identity in the face of persistent systemic exclusion. The theory posits that individuals derive a core sense of self from their affiliation with social groups, which fundamentally shapes their perceptions, behaviors, and capacities for resistance. In repressive contexts, such collective identity not only acts as a psychological buffer against marginalization but also becomes a catalyst for enduring social action, enabling communities like the Bahá'ís to mobilize solidarity, maintain ethical commitments, and assert agency through nonviolent, service-oriented engagement.

For Bahá'ís in Iran, religious identity is inextricably linked to community-building efforts that transcend survivalist strategies and actively contribute to social well-being. Despite facing systemic restrictions on official education and state employment, Bahá'ís, particularly women and youth, have actively pursued grassroots initiatives grounded in Bahá'í principles of service and social transformation. Within Bahá'í thought, the concept of service holds a central and sanctified position, understood not only as a spiritual duty but also as a fundamental expression of faith-based agency and purposeful engagement with the world. Based on Bahá'í thought, I conceptualize service in several interrelated forms. It operates as both an expression of love for humanity and devotion to the Creator, extending beyond selective assistance to include even one's adversaries. Bahá'í teachings also emphasize a balanced life in which service is integrated with material livelihood and spiritual growth. By framing service as a form of worship, Bahá'í theology shifts devotion from ritual practice to an embodied ethical orientation. Thus, service is not merely philanthropic but a transformative force that shapes individual agency and contributes to broader social change.

Service as Love and Devotion

Unlike conventional understandings of service, which may be shaped by duty or personal benefit, the Bahá'í framework emphasizes selfless service rooted in love for humanity and devotion to creator. This spiritualized approach transforms acts of service into dynamic instruments of social change, particularly under conditions of marginalization. "Love and serve mankind just for the sake of God and not for anything else. The foundation of your love toward humanity must be spiritual faith and Divine assurance" ('Abdu'l-Bahá in Hornby 1988, 213). This statement foregrounds the spiritual grounding of service within the Bahá'í tradition, emphasizing that acts of care and solidarity derive their legitimacy not from social expectation or reciprocity but from a theologically anchored commitment to the oneness of humanity. From this perspective, service is understood as an expression of divine love, an outward manifestation of an inner spiritual orientation, rather than a transactional practice oriented toward recognition or reward. Such an understanding aligns with moral motivation theories that highlight the role of transcendent commitments in shaping ethical action, where conduct is guided by alignment with a higher moral order rather than external sanction.

Service Beyond Selectivity

Furthermore, service in the Bahá'í perspective is not limited to aiding those who are receptive or deserving but extends even to one's adversaries. "No, rather he must return good for evil, and not only forgive, but also, if possible, be of service to his oppressor. This conduct is worthy of man" ('Abdu'l-Bahá 1984, 269). This ethical injunction resonates with broader theories of nonviolent resistance and transformative agency. Framing service toward one's oppressor as an ideal aligns with James C. Scott's (1985) notion of "everyday forms of resistance," in which domination is subverted through the preservation of moral autonomy rather than through direct confrontation. It also echoes Hannah Arendt's (1970) understanding of power as arising from ethically grounded action rather than coercion, suggesting that meaningful transformation emerges when individuals refuse to reproduce the logic of violence. Within this framework, 'Abdu'l-Bahá's statement advances a transformative ethic that redefines service as an active interruption of cycles of hostility. Particularly under conditions of systemic oppression, this orientation foregrounds agency as the capacity to act in ways that rehumanize both self and other. In this sense, service functions not merely as a moral virtue but as a socially generative practice that challenges the normative foundations of oppression, reconstituting agency as the ability to expand the moral horizon of the social world.

Service and Integrated Living

Additionally, Bahá'í teachings emphasize the necessity of a balanced life in which service is harmonized with both material advancement and spiritual growth.

> Now I shall tell you the essence of service. Share your time with God. Spend half of the day in search of livelihood, guaranteeing your material life and dignified appearance and dedicate the other half in the acquisition of moral virtues and service at the threshold of God.
>
> ('Abdu'l-Bahá 1927, 365)

This guidance presents a holistic Bahá'í understanding of service by integrating economic self-sufficiency with spiritual development, dissolving the divide between material livelihood and moral cultivation. It frames agency not as resistance alone but as the capacity to align daily practices with a broader ethical orientation, where livelihood enables autonomy and meaningful participation in community life. At the same time, this integration shapes identity, as service becomes an embodied practice through which individuals enact shared values and reinforce collective belonging. In this way, the fusion of work and service constitutes a framework for cultivating both agency and a morally grounded, socially generative identity.

From Ritual to Embodied Service

Moreover, Bahá'í thought conceptualizes service as a form of worship, thereby reconfiguring devotion not as ritualistic observance alone but as embodied ethical practice. This reframing aligns spiritual fulfillment with socially transformative action, blurring the boundary between faith and civic engagement.

> This is worship: to serve mankind and to minister to the needs of the people. Service is prayer. A physician ministering to the sick, gently, tenderly, free from prejudice and believing in the solidarity of the human race, he is giving praise.
>
> (Abdu'l-Bahá 1912/1972, 176–177)

This passage articulates a central Bahá'í redefinition of worship, locating its essence not in ritual observance but in acts of compassionate service. By framing healing, teaching, and ethically grounded labor as forms of prayer,

'Abdu'l-Bahá reconceives devotion as an embodied ethical practice that affirms human dignity and collective well-being. Everyday acts of care are thus elevated to spiritual praxis, collapsing the distinction between sacred and mundane activity.

For Bahá'ís living as a marginalized religious minority, service assumes additional significance, functioning as a resilient practice that sustains moral integrity and collective purpose under structural oppression. Rather than internalizing exclusion, believers enact agency that reaffirms spiritual identity and counters dehumanization, asserting moral subjectivity through constructive social engagement. This ethic of service also underpins communal identity, grounding belonging in practices that embody justice, solidarity, and the oneness of humanity. Social identity theory emphasizes how shared norms and practices shape collective identity; within the Bahá'í community, service functions as both a boundary-marker and an aspirational model of conduct, fostering moral excellence, social contribution, and spiritual resilience over reactive opposition.

Finally, conceiving service as worship reshapes understandings of agency under oppression. Rather than relying on overt resistance, agency emerges through sustained ethical action that nurtures relationships, affirms life, and builds social cohesion. Within constraints, service models an alternative moral order rooted in compassion and justice, demonstrating that spiritual devotion can be a source of moral resilience, minority identity consolidation, and socially generative agency.

Service Beyond Philanthropy

In Bahá'í thought, service is not merely philanthropic or spiritual but a transformative practice that shapes individual agency and fosters social change. In contexts of systemic exclusion, such as the protracted persecution of Bahá'ís in Iran, service performed by Bahá'í individuals, especially women, functions both as a strategy of resilience and an assertion of minority identity. By addressing socioeconomic needs and reinforcing communal values of justice, solidarity, and human dignity, these acts of service enact agency within, and subtly against, the structural constraints imposed upon them. Yet the growing visibility of such initiatives has intensified state repression, with participants, both Bahá'ís and collaborating non-Bahá'ís, subjected to surveillance, arbitrary arrest, and imprisonment. The disproportionately high number of Bahá'í women among detainees underscores the intersectional pressures of gender, religious identity, and authoritarian control, as elaborated in Chapter 1.

Conclusion

This chapter advances a theoretical reframing of agency by positioning the practices of Bahá'í women in Iran as exemplars of a relational, ethically grounded, and spiritually informed mode of resistance. Bringing together feminist theory, intersectionality, agency–structure debates, and social identity theory, it challenges dominant paradigms that equate agency with secular autonomy or confrontational dissent. Instead, it conceptualizes faith-based agency as a form of resistance produced through ethical self-formation, collective responsibility, and community-building practices that operate within, against, and beyond authoritarian constraints. Through a decolonial and interdisciplinary lens, the chapter demonstrates that the social actions of Bahá'í women, education, service, and moral leadership, function as non-adversarial yet politically meaningful interventions. Intersectional analysis reveals how compounded marginalization generates distinctive strategies of resilience, while social identity theory helps illuminate how shared values and communal narratives sustain cohesion under repression. The state's punitive response further underscores the transformative potential of these practices.

The proposed paradox of suppressed alternatives (PSA) conceptualizes this dynamic by arguing that authoritarian regimes suppress not only dissent but viable alternative social imaginaries. The targeting of Bahá'í women signals recognition of the moral and civic possibilities embedded in their communal practices, revealing suppression as an implicit acknowledgment of competing visions of justice and social organization. Overall, the chapter situates the agency of Bahá'í women as a theoretical contribution to minority studies: a model of resistance rooted in spirituality, relationality, and ethical praxis. This framework broadens the analytical vocabulary for understanding how marginalized groups generate pathways to dignity and collective resilience within contexts of systemic repression.

Reference List

AI-assisted tools, including Grammarly, were used for language editing and structural clarity. The author retained full responsibility for the intellectual content of the chapter.

'Abdu'l-Bahá. 1927, March. "The Essence of Service." *Star of the West* 17: 365.

'Abdu'l-Bahá. 1972. *Paris Talks*, 176–177. London: Bahá'í Publishing Trust. (Originally published 1912).

'Abdu'l-Bahá. 1982. *The Promulgation of Universal Peace: Talks Delivered by 'Abdu'l-Bahá during His Visit to the United States and Canada in 1912*. 2nd ed. Wilmette, IL: Bahá'í Publishing Trust. (Originally published 1912).

'Abdu'l-Bahá. 1984. *Some Answered Questions*. Wilmette, IL: Bahá'í Publishing Trust.

'Abdu'l-Bahá. 1988. *Paris Talks*. Wilmette, IL: Bahá'í Publishing Trust.

Ali, Kecia. 2016. *Sexual Ethics and Islam: Feminist Reflections on Qur'an, Hadith, and Jurisprudence*. Oxford: Oneworld Publications. ISBN-10: 1851684565.

Anthias, Floya. 2012. "Transnational Mobilities, Migration Research and Intersectionality: Towards a Translocational Frame." *Nordic Journal of Migration Research* 2 (2): 102–110. https://doi.org/10.2478/v10202-011-0032-y

Arendt, H. 1970. *On Violence*. New York: Harcourt Brace.

Barlas, Asma. 2002. *Believing Women in Islam: Unreading Patriarchal Interpretations of the Qur'an*. Austin, TX: University of Texas Press.

Bilge, Sirma. 2013. "Intersectionality Undone: Saving Intersectionality from Feminist Intersectionality Studies." *Du Bois Review: Social Science Research on Race* 10 (2): 405–424. https://doi.org/10.1017/S1742058X13000283

Bourdieu, Pierre. 1990. *The Logic of Practice*. Stanford, CA: Stanford University Press.

Butler, Judi. 1997. *The Psychic Life of Power: Theories in Subjection*. Stanford University Press.

Chiseri-Strater, Elizabeth. 1996. "Turning In upon Ourselves: Positionality, Subjectivity and Reflexivity in Case Study and Ethnographic Research." In *Ethics and Representation in Qualitative Studies of Literacy*, edited by Peter Mortensen and Gesa E. Kirsch, 115–133. Urbana, IL: National Council of Teachers of English.

Crenshaw, Kimberlé. 1989. "Demarginalizing the Intersection of Race and Sex: A Black Feminist Critique of Antidiscrimination Doctrine, Feminist Theory, and Antiracist Politics." *University of Chicago Legal Forum* 1989 (1): 139–167.

Erevelles, Nirmala, and Andrea Minear. 2010. "Unspeakable Offenses: Untangling Race and Disability in Discourses of Intersectionality." *Journal of Literary & Cultural Disability Studies* 4 (2): 127–145. https://doi.org/10.3828/jlcds.2010.11.

Foucault, Michel. 1991. *The Foucault Effect: Studies in Governmentality*, edited by Graham Burchell, Colin Gordon, and Peter Miller. Chicago, IL: University of Chicago Press.

Giddens, Anthony. 1984. *The Constitution of Society: Outline of the Theory of Structuration*. Berkeley: University of California Press.

Hornby, Helen Bassett, comp. 1988. *Lights of Guidance: A Bahá'í Reference File*. New Delhi: Bahá'í Publishing Trust. https://bahai-library.com/hornby_lights_guidance

Karlberg, Michael. 2010. Constructive Resilience: The Bahá'í Response to Oppression. *Peace & Change* 35 (2): 222–257. https://doi.org/10.1111/j.1468-0130.2009.00627.x.

Mahmood, Saba. 2005. *Politics of Piety: The Islamic Revival and the Feminist Subject*. Princeton, NJ: Princeton University Press.

Mohammad, Robina. 2001. "Insiders and/or Outsiders: Positionality, Theory and Praxis." In *Qualitative Methods for Geographers: Issues and Debates*, edited by Melanie Limb and Claire Dwyer, 101–117. Oxford: Oxford University Press.

Mohanty, Chandra Talpade. 2003. *Feminism without Borders: Decolonizing Theory, Practicing Solidarity*. Durham, NC: Duke University Press.

Rahimi (Mottahedeh), Pouran. 2011. *Eshgh be Baha-ye Jan [عشق به بهای جان]*. USA: Baha'i National Center.

Scott, James C. 1985. *Weapons of the Weak: Everyday Forms of Peasant Resistance*. New Haven, CT: Yale University Press.

Scott, James C. 1990. *Domination and the Arts of Resistance: Hidden Transcripts*. New Haven, CT: Yale University Press.

Shoghi Effendi. 1933. "Letter Written on Behalf of Shoghi Effendi, February 17, 1933." In *Compilation of Compilations, Vol. 1, Social and Economic Development*, 4. Mona Vale, NSW: Bahá'í Publications Australia.

Tajfel, Henri, and John C. Turner. 1979. "An Integrative Theory of Intergroup Conflict." In *The Social Psychology of Intergroup Relations*, edited by William G. Austin and Stephen Worchel, 33–47. Monterey, CA: Brooks/Cole.

Universal House of Justice. 1996. *The Universal House of Justice, 1963–1986: The Third Epoch of the Formative Age*. Wilmette, IL: Bahá'í Publishing Trust. https://bahai-library.com/uhj_messages_1963_1986

Wadud, Amina. 2006. *Inside the Gender Jihad: Women's Reform in Islam*. Oxford: Oneworld Publications. ISBN: 9781851684632.

2 From Oppression to Emancipation

Bahá'í Women and the Woman, Life, Freedom Movement in Iran

Introduction

The first section of this chapter will explore the historical timeline of events in Iran from September 2022 to spring 2025, a period marked by nearly 27 months of significant upheavals and transformations within Iran, the Middle East, and globally. The rapid pace of change, particularly in Iran, has been unprecedented, with the population witnessing a cascade of political, social, and economic shifts. The second section will focus on events specifically impacting the Bahá'í community, presented through a historical timeline with a particular emphasis on the Bahá'í women facing discrimination and the strategies of resistance they employed within and beyond traditional spaces. This section will include the life narratives of two Bahá'í women who faced severe persecution during this period, illustrating the resilience and agency demonstrated in the face of systemic oppression.

Finally, the chapter will reflect on the broader implications of Iranian women's resilience for social movements and collective action both within Iran and across the diaspora. Drawing from my personal experiences, I will analyze how these dynamics contribute to the evolving landscape of resistance, solidarity, and the pursuit of justice in the face of ongoing adversity. The sources of information for this chapter are diverse, encompassing both primary and secondary materials. They include media reports from public and personal accounts, official publications from the Bahá'í International Community's website, and content from social media platforms such as YouTube, Twitter, and Instagram, both from individuals and official or unofficial organizations. Additionally, the chapter draws on newspaper articles, academic literature, and my personal experiences gained through participation in various events regarding the WLF uprising. Supplementary data has been gathered through extensive internet searches to ensure a comprehensive understanding of the subject matter.

A Historical Glimpse of Resistance and Repression (September 2022–January 2025)

The historical overview presented in this section does not aim to provide an exhaustive account of all events. Rather, it seeks to offer a broad perspective

DOI: 10.4324/9781003567370-3

that highlights key developments, illustrating patterns of repression, state violence, and the corresponding resistance and protests, particularly as manifested among Iranian women and the younger generation. The focus is on capturing the essence of these dynamics to convey a clear understanding of the sociopolitical landscape during this period.

On 3 August 2021, Sayyid Ebrahim Raisi,[1] a politically conservative Muslim jurist, was elected the eighth president of Iran while the people of Iran were still seething from Aban Protests.[2] Large-scale protests continued throughout the country in late 2022 in response to strong distrust and dissatisfaction with government programs, tumbling economic collapse, corruption in governmental organizations, brutal repression, and the violation of the rights of women and ethnic and religious minorities. The current uprising starting on 16 September 2022 brought about by the tragic death of Mahsa Amini, age 22, was on 13 September 2022 when she was arrested for improper use of Hijab[3] and brought by the morality police,[4] a unit of Iran's police force established under former hardline president Ahmadinejad,[5] to their headquarters and died in custody. Amini's death deeply aggravated the nation igniting a countrywide uprising in which women are evident in both quality and quantity. The state's refusal to look into the causes of her death or offer an apology further extended the protesters' anger. Demonstrators soon began to chant, "Don't be scared, don't be scared, we are all together," "Death to the dictator," and "Death to the Islamic Republic."[6] The recent uprising in Iran must also be understood as a broader public response to the regime's pervasive corruption, aggressive foreign policy, and regional expansionism, all of which have deepened Iran's international isolation and exacerbated the country's economic collapse, notably through soaring inflation (Harders, Jünemann and Khatib 2017). What

1 Sayyid Ebrahim Raisi, better known as Ebrahim Raisi, was an Iranian politician who served as the eighth president of Iran from 2021 until his death in a helicopter crash in 2024. He was a Muslim jurist and part of the Principlist group.

2 The 2019–2020 Iranian protests, also known as Bloody November or Bloody Aban (Persian: آبان خونین), were nationwide demonstrations sparked by a 50–200% increase in fuel prices. Initially peaceful on 15 November 2019, the protests quickly spread to over 21 cities, fueled by social media, and evolved into demands for the overthrow of the government and Supreme Leader Ali Khamenei. They became the most violent unrest in Iran since the 1979 Revolution.

3 https://www.gettyimages.fi/photos/mahsa-amini

4 Islamic religious police, also known as morality police or sharia police, are official law enforcement agencies in some Muslim-majority countries. They enforce religious observance and public morality based on their interpretation of sharīʿah, operating under the authority of national or regional governments (Cordesman 2003).

5 Mahmoud Ahmadinejad is an Iranian Principlist and nationalist politician who served as the sixth president of Iran from 2005 to 2013. He is currently a member of the Expediency Discernment Council. Known for his hardline stance, his presidency was marked by economic challenges, heightened tensions with the West, and the advancement of Iran's nuclear program.

6 These slogans have repeated since 2009. https://www.nytimes.com/2009/06/21/opinion/21tehran.html

makes this moment particularly distinctive is the entanglement of diverse grievances, ranging from economic hardship to demands for fundamental political freedoms, creating an unprecedented convergence of dissent across socioeconomic, ethnic, and religious lines (Packer 2022).

The eruption of public anger in Iran can be traced, in part, to events preceding Mahsa Amini's death, notably the July 2022 arrest of Sepideh Rashnu. Her detention, following the circulation of a video showing her confrontation with a veiled woman over mandatory hijab laws, underscored escalating tensions over state-imposed dress codes and revealed deepening fractures within Iranian society regarding individual rights and state authority.[7] Shortly thereafter, national television broadcast Rashnu's coerced confession, during which visible facial bruises, clear signs of torture, were prominently displayed. This spectacle sent an unambiguous warning to opponents of compulsory hijab policies.[8] It was not the first time the Iranian government employed forced confessions on national television as a tactic to assert authority, discredit dissent, and suppress activism. Such broadcasts have historically served to intimidate the public and delegitimize political opposition. In the aftermath, the presence of the morality police expanded significantly, leading to a surge in violent arrests of women. Numerous incidents of brutality were captured on video and disseminated across social media platforms, intensifying public outrage and amplifying demands for systemic reform.

The death of Mahsa Amini quickly became a catalyst for widespread outrage. Images of her lifeless body and heartbroken parents circulated rapidly across social media, drawing intense public empathy and transforming her name into a powerful hashtag symbolizing resistance. Her widely shared funeral footage embodied public anger toward the Islamic Republic's oppressive policies.[9] What set this uprising apart from previous movements was the immediate and widespread solidarity with Amini, particularly among Iranians and women across diverse social backgrounds, both inside and outside the country.[10]

Woman, Life, Freedom, the identifying slogan[11] of this uprising, was heard for the first time at Mahsa Amini's funeral and later reverberated worldwide as

7 https://iranwire.com/en/women/105802-woman-arrested-after-fight-with-informant-on-a-bus/

8 https://iranwire.com/en/women/106223-state-tv-airs-forced-confession-by-anti-forced-hijab/

9 https://socialistmiddleeast.com/the-rage-in-iran-is-growing-over-the-murder-of-mahsa-amini

10 Around 80,000 people, including thousands of Iranians, rallied in Berlin on Saturday, the largest of several global protests supporting Iran's women-led movement. Similar demonstrations occurred in cities across Europe, North America, and beyond. https://www.voanews.com/a/thousands-rally-in-berlin-elsewhere-in-support-of-iranian-women-/6801188.html

11 This slogan, originating in the Kurdish-inhabited area, was used by the Kurdish women's movement in 1987 and became popular in other global protests. It was used on 25 November 2015, for example, in gatherings in several European countries to mark International Day for the Elimination of Violence against Women. The slogan created waves of reactions and reflection to the protesters' demands both inside and outside Iran.

a symbol of identifying with the protesters. Women were at the forefront of the protests, removing their Hijabs while dancing, throwing their headscarves into a fire, and singing songs that echoed their demands.[12] The political landscape of Iranian cities shifted dramatically when women appeared in public without hijab. Social media became a pivotal tool, rapidly disseminating images and videos of school and university students, alongside women of all ages, engaging in acts of collective agency. These visuals galvanized broader segments of society, with men and other social groups soon joining the demonstrations across cities. Initially, the government remained silent, expecting the protests to dissipate. However, the rapid spread and persistence of the uprising revealed a profound, nationwide rejection of the Islamic regime's authority.

Ultimately, the regime responded with a heavy-handed crackdown, arresting thousands of protesters, including teenagers. Yet despite the repression, protesters persisted through diverse acts of resistance, chanting the names of slain youths and uniting their voices with the slogan, "Don't be afraid, we are all together," signaling enduring solidarity and embodied agency.[13] Some protesters gathered in front of prisons, demanding the release of political prisoners and those recently detained. The regime forces appeared on the streets with war machines and weapons to confront the protesters and targeted the eyes of the protesters.[14] Young protesters courageously faced state violence, often losing their eyes or even their lives, yet refusing to retreat or abandon the public spaces they had claimed for dissent.

Young women stood courageously before heavily armed officers, removing their headscarves and casting them aside in acts of visible agency. Others cut their hair, invoking an ancient Iranian mourning ritual that symbolizes deep sorrow, anger, new life, and rebirth.[15] This powerful form of dissent quickly captured global attention, creating a resonant symbol of solidarity. The Iranian diaspora played a critical role in amplifying this gesture, as thousands of women worldwide shared videos of themselves cutting their hair across social media platforms, further spreading the movement's message to celebrities, politicians, and activists.[16] The release of a song described as the

12 https://www.bbc.com/news/world-middle-east-62967381

13 The targeting of young people comes amid a broader crackdown on protesters in which 14,000 people have been arrested, according to the United Nations. https://www.nytimes.com/2022/11/14/world/middleeast/iran-protests-children.html

14 The crackdown on nationwide protests in Iran has resulted in over 500 deaths and thousands of injuries. In November, over 370 ophthalmologists reported numerous protesters suffering eye injuries from rubber bullets, metal pellets, and paintball bullets, with over 500 cases of blindness since mid-September due to the use of shotgun birdshots and similar projectiles by security forces. https://www.iranintl.com/en/202302040763

15 https://telegrafi.com/en/grate-iraniane-dhe-gjere-presin-floket-ne-shenje-proteste-per-vdekjen-e-22-vjecares-mahsa-amini/, https://edition.cnn.com/2022/09/28/middleeast/iran-hair-cutting-mime-intl/index.html

16 https://www.latimes.com/california/story/2022-10-06/la-me-iran-protests-diaspora

"anthem" of this protests, called "Baraye" by Shervin Hajipoir[17] has received worldwide acclaim. Again, on 1 October 2022 "Baraye" was sung in approximately 150 cities worldwide as a sign of global solidarity and unity with the Iranian women.[18]

Over the 27 months following the death of Mahsa Amini, Iran witnessed an escalation of state-sponsored repression, characterized by a sharp increase in executions[19] and mass incarcerations. The crackdown targeted a wide spectrum of society, including activists, mothers and fathers[20] seeking for justice, students, academics, doctors, teachers, bus drivers, workers, musicians, artists, lawyers, and journalists, essentially anyone perceived as a threat to the regime. This period was also marked by the expansion of surveillance mechanisms,[21] reflecting the state's efforts to exert tighter control over public and private spheres, suppress dissent, and stifle any form of resistance.

Paradoxically, these oppressive measures have fostered both domestic and transnational solidarity among Iranians, significantly undermining the regime's perceived legitimacy. Despite the pervasive climate of fear, acts of epistemic agency, particularly by women opposing the compulsory hijab, have become increasingly visible through widespread documentation on social media platforms.[22] While these persistent acts of civil disobedience have prompted minor policy adjustments, such as selective relaxation of dress code

17 In 2023, Hajipour won the first Grammy Award for Best Song for Social Change at the 65th Annual Grammy Awards for "Baraye." *Time* magazine named him one of the 100 most influential people in the world in 2023. He was arrested on 29 September 2022, two days after "Baraye" was initially published, and was released on bail on 4 October 2022. https://www.youtube.com/watch?v=0th9_v-BbUI

18 https://en.wikipedia.org/wiki/Timeline_of_the_Mahsa_Amini_protests

19 In 2024, Iran carried out at least 901 executions, marking the highest number recorded in the past nine years and a 6% increase from 2023, when 853 individuals were executed, according to the UN human rights chief, Volker Türk. This alarming rise included around 40 executions in a single week in December. Türk condemned the trend, stating that it is "deeply disturbing" to witness such an increase year after year, and urged Iran to halt this "ever-swelling tide of executions." The majority of executions were related to drug offenses, but individuals connected to the 2022 protests and political dissidents were also among those executed. Notably, there was a significant rise in the number of women executed, with at least 31 women put to death in 2024 – the highest figure since Norway-based Iran Human Rights (IHR) began monitoring executions 17 years ago. https://iranhr.net/en/articles/7263/, https://www.bbc.com/news/articles/ced8qw8q62jo, https://www.ohchr.org/en/press-releases/2025/01/iran-rise-executions-deeply-troubling-un-human-rights-chief

20 https://en.wikipedia.org/wiki/Iranian_Complainant_Mothers,https://www.theguardian.com/world/article/2024/may/25/iran-jails-father-of-young-man-executed-over-2022-protests, https://iranwire.com/en/women/134297-slain-iranian-bloggers-mother-faces-surveillance-after-protest-threat/

21 https://www.state.gov/wp-content/uploads/2024/02/528267_IRAN-2023-HUMAN-RIGHTS-REPORT.pdf, https://www.hrw.org/world-report/2024/country-chapters/iran

22 https://www.rferl.org/a/iran-hijab-insurer-companies-violators-women-rights/32527986.html, https://apnews.com/article/iran-hijab-protests-mahsa-amini-anniversary-59641e9254e-ea45c069b54d590c7e818, https://www.iranintl.com/en/202411032114, https://www.amnesty.org.au/iran-new-compulsory-veiling-law-intensifies-oppression-of-women-and-girls/

enforcement in certain urban areas, the state continues to exert stringent control through pervasive surveillance and targeted acts of violence.

One of the compelling examples of the resilience of Iranian women is the case of a young woman in late 2024, who posted a video of herself singing without wearing a hijab on her YouTube channel.[23] The video quickly went viral, amassing millions of views and receiving widespread praise from both Iranians and global activists. This act of agency against the state's mandatory hijab law,[24] coupled with the recording of a woman's voice singing revolutionary and popular songs, banned as Haram for the past 40 years, embodied the unwavering spirit of resistance within the Iranian women's movement.

Her bold challenge to entrenched patriarchal and authoritarian structures not only disrupted the regime's control over gender norms but also contributed meaningfully to the broader transnational struggle for gender equality and personal freedoms. Moreover, her artistic act underscores the pivotal role of digital platforms in amplifying grassroots dissent, transforming individual expressions of resistance into collective symbols of empowerment that transcend national boundaries (Keck and Sikkink 1998). Inspired by her agency, many young women began recording and sharing their own performances

23 Iranian singer Parastoo Ahmadi was hailed as a symbol of agency by supporters after performing an online concert without wearing a hijab, challenging the Islamic Republic's strict dress code. The concert, streamed on her YouTube channel in December 2024, featured Ahmadi in a long, flowing black dress with bare shoulders and no headscarf. She performed alongside a four-man band playing keyboard, percussion, and guitars on an outdoor stage set within the grounds of a traditional caravanserai complex in Iran. No live audience was present. Since the 1979 Islamic Revolution, Iranian law has mandated that women cover their hair in public and prohibits them from singing solo in public spaces. Despite these restrictions, Ahmadi has gained a significant following through her Instagram, where she posts ballads recorded indoors without a headscarf, often in support of the 2022–2023 mass protests against the regime. These protests were ignited by the death of 22-year-old Mahsa Amini. Ahmadi's recent performance marked the first time she publicly recorded a full concert outdoors, contrasting with her previous intimate, indoor recordings. Before the concert began, a message appeared on the screen: "I am Parastoo, the girl who cannot remain silent and refuses to stop singing for the country she loves." In one of her songs, she poignantly references the violent crackdowns on protesters: "From the blood of the youth of the homeland, tulips have grown." https://www.hindustantimes.com/world-news/iranian-singer-who-performed-without-hijab-to-face-appropriate-action-judiciary-says-101734159571097.html

24 The Hijab and Chastity Law (officially titled *The Law to Support the Family by Promoting the Culture of Chastity and Hijab*) is the principal regulation enforcing mandatory hijab in Iran, passed by the Islamic Consultative Assembly in November 2024. This bill was drafted by the Iranian judiciary following the dissolution of the Guidance Patrol and amid the Women, Life, Freedom movement. It was subsequently submitted to the Islamic Consultative Assembly by the administration of President Seyyed Ebrahim Raisi. The newspaper *Etemad* reported that the implementation of this law could effectively criminalize half of the country's population. https://www.etemadonline.com/. However, the compulsory hijab has been imposed by the state and has remained a central point of contention between women and the government.

on personal social media accounts, further reinforcing a digitally mediated network of solidarity and resistance.

The individual and collective agency and resilience of Iranian women in the face of systemic repression have catalyzed a transformative shift within both national and transnational resistance movements. Drawing on social movement theory (Tarrow 1998; Della Porta and Diani 2006) and frameworks of transnational activism (Keck and Sikkink 1998), this resilience may be conceptualized as a form of transnational agency, simultaneously confronting entrenched patriarchal and authoritarian structures within Iran while mobilizing solidarity across diasporic and global civil society. The increasing visibility of Iranian women's agency, amplified through digital platforms, international media, and grassroots mobilization, has contributed to the formation of a shared collective consciousness among Iranians in exile and their allies. In turn, these transnational networks generate discursive and political pressures that complicate the state's capacity to fully suppress dissent and isolate opposition. Localized acts of resistance thus become interconnected nodes within a broader matrix of advocacy, illustrating the disruptive potential of networked activism and underscoring the dynamic interplay between internal protest and external support.

As a human rights advocate, scholar, and former political prisoner who has endured systemic discrimination as a member of the Bahá'í community in Iran, my engagement with social movements is shaped by both critical inquiry and lived experience. Since the 2022 uprising, this engagement has intensified: I have participated in international seminars, activist forums, and transnational coalitions working to amplify the voices of Iranian women and political dissidents. In Turku, Finland, I have helped organize weekly public demonstrations to show solidarity with political prisoners and victims of state violence, distributing documentation of human rights abuses often overlooked by Western media.[25] Our efforts have brought attention to the plight of poisoned schoolgirls, women murdered in so-called "honor killings," executed protesters, and grieving "Mothers of Justice."

These acts of resistance are not theoretical abstractions, they are immediate, personal, and deeply felt. For many in the diaspora, Iran remains an emotional homeland, continuously inhabited through mourning and activism. Despite repression, activists in exile have forged an unprecedented unity across political, ethnic, and religious lines. Personally, I dedicate multiple evenings each week to analyzing current events, creating media content, writing, and organizing civic programming with other Iranian activists around the world.[26] Having been engaged in activism since 1998, I can attest that today's

25 https://www.instagram.com/wlf_turku/

26 Regional Coordinator (Europe) of the International Community of Iranian Academics (ICOIA) https://icoia.org/, Center For Human Rights In Iran https://bashariyat.org/, Global Campaign

convergence of diverse voices marks a historic and transformative moment in the collective struggle for justice and structural change in Iran.

Bahá'í Women and the Woman, Life, Freedom Movement

In contexts of state-sponsored violence, minority communities are often subjected to intensified forms of repression (Karlberg 2010). In Iran, the WLF movement has produced both repressive and generative effects on the Bahá'í community, particularly among women. While many Iranian women have participated in public protests, numerous Bahá'í women, guided by principles of non-confrontation, have refrained from demonstrations, yet have nonetheless faced arrest and systemic discrimination solely based on their religious identity, which the state frames as inherently oppositional to Islam, as outlined in the Introduction.[27]

This state-driven representation stands in stark contrast to the foundational principles of the Bahá'í Faith, which emphasize the unity of religions, the oneness of the Creator, and the continuity of divine revelation through successive prophets.[28] Moreover, Bahá'ís are explicitly prohibited from engaging in partisan political activity or affiliating with opposition movements (Smith 2008; Bahá'í International Community 2005). Rather, they are encouraged to demonstrate loyalty to the government under which they reside while contributing to social development and public discourse and advancing justice and equality within society.[29]

Paradoxically, intensified discrimination, particularly against Bahá'í women, has increased the community's visibility and engagement. This has enabled Bahá'ís to reconnect with broader Iranian society and to reframe their identity as agents of social transformation committed to justice, gender equality, and collective well-being, thereby challenging state narratives that cast them as subversive. As a Bahá'í woman in exile, I have both observed and contributed to this reconfiguration of resistance through public demonstrations, international advocacy, and engagement with diverse activist networks. My academic and activist work aims to contribute to foregrounding the role

---

No to Executions in Iran https://www.iranintl.com/202504085263, Women Life Freedom Global Network https://www.womanlifefreedom.today/, Amnesty Turku Local Group Coordinator https://www.instagram.com/amnestyturku/, and WLF Turku https://www.instagram.com/wlf_turku/

27 For more information read this report by Diane Ala'i, a Representative of the Bahá'í International Community to the United Nations in Geneva. https://www.bic.org/perspectives/perspective-70-years-udhr-have-human-rights-mechanisms-protected-bahai-community-iran,

28 More information about Bahá'íFaith. https://www.bic.org/statements/faith-bahaullah-world-religion and https://www.britannica.com/topic/Bahai-Faith

29 https://www.bahai.org/library/authoritative-texts/the-universal-house-of-justice/messages/20170427_001/1#660111388, https://bahaipedia.org/Politics, https://bahaiworld.bahai.org/library/the-pursuit-of-social-justice/

of Bahá'í women within Iran's broader human rights movement, challenging their historical marginalization and fostering intersectional solidarity through scholarly publications, conferences, seminars, media engagement, and digital platforms that amplify marginalized voices.

The Intensified Repression of Bahá'í Women Amid Iran's Current Political Unrest

Drawing on personal experience as a target of state repression, this section examines the intensified persecution of Bahá'í women within Iran's broader resistance movement. It first examines how the Islamic government has falsely linked the Bahá'í community, particularly women, to the protests to justify intensified repression. Drawing on human rights reports and Bahá'í International Community (BIC) archives, it documents the rise in arrests and detentions and highlights the experiences of two Bahá'í women as emblematic of resilience.

Ten days after the death of Mahsa Amini, on 26 September 2022, the Special Rapporteurs on Iran, freedom of religion, and minorities condemned the "systematic" persecution of Bahá'ís in Iran. They emphasized that while this persecution has spanned over four decades, recent months have seen an unprecedented escalation, reminiscent of the early years of the Islamic Revolution when efforts to eliminate the Bahá'í community were in full force. The rapporteurs noted that in the past six weeks alone, 274 incidents of persecution have occurred, including arrests, property destruction, confiscations, beatings, and raids. Furthermore, over 100 young Bahá'ís have been denied access to higher education,[30] continuing a long-standing pattern of discrimination.[31]

On 8 December 2022, a cleric affiliated with a radical Islamist faction publicly sought to delegitimize the WLF movement by linking it to the Bahá'í community. In a statement published by a state-aligned newspaper, Hojjat al-Islam Ahmad Hossein Falahi, Hamedan's representative in the 11th Iranian Parliament, claimed that "unveiled women without scarves are Bahá'ís." He further asserted that those who now appear unveiled have "always been this

30 Bahá'í youth who pursue alternative avenues for education face persistent harassment by Iranian authorities. Denied access to universities, many Bahá'ís attend classes in private homes through the Bahá'í Institute of Higher Education (BIHE), an informal educational initiative established to provide higher education opportunities to those systematically excluded. However, in February 2024, intelligence agents raided the home of Mrs. Zabihi, where a BIHE exam was being conducted, confiscating textbooks and other materials. During the raid, agents subjected Mrs. Zabihi to verbal abuse and physical intimidation. When her young son protested their actions, he was violently beaten in front of his mother. https://www.bic.org/focus-areas/situation-iranian-bahais/current-situation, https://www.bic.org/news/iranian-agents-beat-bahai-youth-during-attack-educational-group-and-knowledge-itself

31 https://www.bic.org/statements/statement-un-human-rights-council-51st-session-situation-bahais-iran

way," and that among them are individuals belonging to the so-called "deviant Bahá'í sect," which, according to him, has long promoted unveiling. Falahi accused the Bahá'í community of not only orchestrating efforts against the hijab but also engaging in espionage for the Zionist regime, calling upon security agencies to exercise heightened vigilance.[32] Falahi further emphasized that unveiled women are not Muslims and argued that, from a legal and security standpoint, their actions require more serious intervention by security institutions.[33]

A few months later in 11 January 2023, the same newspaper addressed the issue of "why Bahá'ís do not have equal rights with other citizens." Referring to another publication,[34] it provided a response, highlighting specific justifications for the differential treatment: Based on Islamic governance and Sharia law, Iran's political system establishes different legal frameworks for various religious groups. While Shia and Sunni Muslims have specific rulings, minorities like Christians, Jews, and Zoroastrians are recognized with distinct regulations. Followers of non-recognized religions, such as the Bahá'í Faith, are not granted equal rights, only basic human rights like fair trials and protection from torture. The government's treatment of non-recognized sects varies. Groups like Buddhists, who do not oppose the Islamic regime, are not targeted, but sects such as the Bahá'í Faith, which oppose the regime and collaborate with its enemies, face restrictions. The Bahá'ís have historically opposed the Islamic Republic and continue to cooperate with Israel, leading to their exclusion from equal rights under the Constitution and legal regulations.[35]

Such statements exemplify the Islamic Republic's broader strategy of *religio-political othering*, wherein dissent is framed as a deviation not only from national loyalty but from religious orthodoxy. By constructing protesters as existential outsiders to both the moral order and the imagined national community, the regime employs a discursive mechanism of exclusion that serves to delegitimize political resistance. This strategy functions as a justification for escalated repression, aligning with what Foucault (1991) terms *governmentality*, a form of power that regulates populations by pathologizing dissent and rendering alternative subjectivities illegible within the dominant ideological framework.

In a document released in December 2023 (almost 15 months after the death of Mahsa Amini), the BIC highlighted that the period leading up to that date had been characterized by a troubling intensification of the persecution

32 https://eghtesaad24.ir/fa/news/177395/, 2022 December 8

33 Translated from a Persian document https://iranbahaipersecution.bic.org/fa/archive/aqtsad-24-znan-hjab-kh-shal-w-rwsry-ndarnd-bhayy-hstnd, 2022 December 8

34 https://www.javanonline.ir/

35 Translated into Persian. https://eghtesaad24.ir/fa/news/181100/

of the Bahá'í community in Iran.[36] A systematic campaign of home invasions, arbitrary arrests, and abusive treatment has unfolded across various cities, beginning with Shiraz and extending to Yazd, Isfahan, Hamedan, Karaj, and Shirvan.[37] Since October 2023, approximately 40 Bahá'ís have been arrested, and the homes of nearly 100 families have been subjected to invasive searches.[38] In Hamedan, armed and masked agents forcibly entered the homes of 33 families, many of which housed elderly women, including individuals in their eighties suffering from chronic illnesses such as Alzheimer's.[39] Security forces used excessive force, breaking windows and doors to gain entry, leading to the hospitalization of several elderly individuals due to trauma-induced health crises, including one heart attack that required emergency resuscitation.[40]

A particularly concerning development is the disproportionate targeting of Bahá'í women, who make up a significant majority of those detained in

36 https://www.bic.org/statements/change-tactics-iranian-governments-recent-persecution-bahais

37 In October 2023, 10 women from Isfahan, mostly in their twenties and thirties, were arrested. In the same month, 26 Bahá'ís, 16 of them women, received sentences totaling 126 years in prison, signaling the continued targeting of women across the Bahá'í community. A month later, in November 2023, 6 more Bahá'í women from Isfahan were detained for one month, facing harsh conditions in the quarantine ward of Dolat Abad prison. Deliberate delays in giving them medical care, restricted access to warm water, and the denial of information about the reasons for their arrests, or the charges against them, highlight the troubling rise in the Iranian government's harsh new tactics against Bahá'í women. https://www.bic.org/focus-areas/situation-iranian-bahais/current-situation

38 One of the most distressing trends has been the violent and degrading treatment inflicted upon Bahá'ís by security forces during these raids. Reports indicate numerous cases of physical and psychological abuse both during home invasions and subsequent interrogations in detention centers. For instance, in one city, security agents severely beat a young boy in front of his family after he protested the aggressive search of their home. In another case, a woman returning from dropping her child at school was forcibly thrown into her home by plainclothes agents who proceeded to conduct an unauthorized search. Similarly, a father suffered a heart attack during a raid as his daughter was being taken into custody. https://www.bic.org/statements/change-tactics-iranian-governments-recent-persecution-bahais

39 In November 2023, due to extreme stress as a result of home raids, an elderly lady was taken to a heart clinic by ambulance and another was transferred to the Intensive Care Unit. Another became seriously ill and suffered a mild stroke, requiring resuscitation by paramedics. Additionally, one elderly lady suffering from Alzheimer's disease, faced aggression and intimidation during a raid. The home of an 82-year-old woman was forcefully broken down, her belongings searched and upended and her residence damaged in her absence. https://www.bic.org/focus-areas/situation-iranian-bahais/current-situation

40 The scope of these operations extends beyond physical raids. Homes have been ransacked, with agents destroying personal property, including furniture and musical instruments. In some cases, they installed surveillance cameras to monitor Bahá'í families and their visitors. Victims of these raids have faced threats of severe repercussions should they disclose details of their experiences. Authorities have systematically deleted evidence, including smartphone footage and CCTV recordings, to obscure the extent of their actions. https://www.bic.org/statements/change-tactics-iranian-governments-recent-persecution-bahais

2024.[41] Many of these women are in their twenties and thirties and have been forcibly separated from their young children. Raids often occurred in the presence of children, exacerbating the psychological trauma inflicted on families. Notable cases include a young woman sentenced to five years in prison simply for inquiring about her grandmother's burial, thereby being separated from her 5-year-old daughter.[42] Another woman, a mother of two, received a ten-year prison sentence after enduring a year of pre-trial detention.[43] According to the BIC's analysis of 2021–2023, the overall persecution of Bahá'ís in Iran has intensified by approximately 50% each year since 2021.[44]

Similar reports published in December 2024[45] and January 2025[46] indicate that the situation of the Bahá'í community, particularly women, has deteriorated further. The Iranian government continues to incarcerate, expel from universities, dismiss from employment, and persecute Bahá'í women for their aspiration to live as equals, working alongside others, regardless of gender, background, or belief, in their efforts to contribute to the progress of their country. Amid a broad spectrum of human rights violations against the Bahá'í community, particularly women, recent reports highlight specific areas of concern. By mid-2024, 72 out of the 93 Bahá'ís summoned to court or imprisoned were women, accounting for more than three quarters of those persecuted.[47]

41 https://www.agenciaflama.cat/wp-content/uploads/DownLoadPublicCommunicationFile.pdf, https://www.bic.org/news/eighteen-un-experts-jointly-and-unitedly-condemn-irans-targeting-bahai-women-10-isfahan-are-sentenced-total-90-years-prison

42 https://iranpresswatch.org/post/24027/the-ir-has-extended-suppression-to-cemeteries-and-funerals/

43 Many detainees remain in custody without trial, some for extended periods exceeding 247 days, and are denied bail. The charges levied against them are often baseless, such as "membership in the deviant Bahá'í sect" or "engaging in social activities to promote the heretical Bahá'í sect." Courts have imposed harsh sentences for humanitarian activities, including teaching underprivileged children and providing disaster relief. Currently, at least 70 Bahá'ís are either detained or serving prison sentences – the highest number in six years. Additionally, around 1,200 individuals face ongoing legal proceedings or are awaiting imprisonment following sentencing. Sentences have become increasingly severe, with cumulative prison terms amounting to hundreds of years in recent weeks. Bahá'ís released on bail face exorbitant financial demands, with bail amounts ranging from 20 to 80 times the annual salary of a government employee. For example, a young woman in Shiraz was required to post bail equivalent to nearly USD 200,000 – an insurmountable sum for most Iranian families. https://www.bic.org/statements/change-tactics-iranian-governments-recent-persecution-bahais

44 https://www.bic.org/focus-areas/situation-iranian-bahais/current-situation

45 https://www.iranrights.org/attachments/library/doc_1165.pdf, https://www.iranintl.com/en/202411118773, https://reliefweb.int/report/iran-islamic-republic/iran-experts-alarmed-systematic-targeting-bahai-women

46 https://www.bic.org/news/125-european-parliamentarians-join-un-experts-condemn-escalating-persecution-iranian-bahai-women. This document released today, 6 February 2025 while I am writing this chapter. https://iranhrdc.org/a-faith-denied-the-persecution-of-the-bahais-of-iran/

47 https://www.iranintl.com/en/202407048545, https://shafaq.com/en/World/Iran-sentences-15-Bah-women-to-75-years-in-prison

A central question guiding this section is why Bahá'í women have faced disproportionately high rates of detention, imprisonment, and targeting during the current wave of protests in Iran. Emerging evidence, along with my personal experience, indicates that these state actions are not merely reactive responses to conventional political dissent, but rather reflect a broader strategy aimed at suppressing grassroots social development efforts that challenge hegemonic control. Bahá'í women's involvement in community-based initiatives, including informal education for children and youth, empowerment workshops for women, counseling, coaching, yoga instruction, and advocacy through writing or social media platforms such as Instagram and Facebook, has been systematically reframed by the Iranian state as ideological subversion.[48]

From the perspective of the regime, these activities constitute a disruption of state authority, despite their non-partisan and service-oriented foundations. Drawing on Nancy Fraser's (1995) concept of counter public and subaltern counter-hegemony,[49] such practices, however modest or community-based, can be interpreted as politically generative. They represent forms of civic agency that generate alternative, discursive and material spaces for empowerment, dignity, and collective subjectivity, thereby unsettling the dominant political order.

This conceptual argument is grounded in lived experience. Between 2006 and 2010, I was held in solitary confinement for four years for organizing social development programs in underprivileged neighborhoods in Shiraz. These initiatives, which included more than 70 Bahá'í and Muslim youth volunteers, offered educational support to children neglected from Iran's stratified and ideologically controlled public education system.[50] Despite being apolitical and framed as service-oriented, these programs were criminalized and treated as threats to state ideology and national security of the country. The pattern of repression has persisted beyond national borders. In exile, my continued advocacy for social justice, academic freedom, gender equality, and inclusive civic discourse has elicited targeted harassment by state-affiliated

48 Some Bahá'í women and youth have received calls from security police or been summoned by intelligence services in their cities, where they were threatened simply for being active on Instagram or Twitter. For example, see this https://iranwire.com/en/bahais-of-iran/70278/. After both of them were released, I contacted them and listened to their experiences. Through them, I learned that some Bahá'ís who went through similar situations preferred not to speak about it publicly. Therefore, it is likely that there are more cases, but no online records are available for reference.

49 As she argues in her theory of "counter publics," marginalized groups often engage in everyday practices that challenge dominant discourses, thereby becoming political by virtue of their visibility and social impact. Fraser, N. (1995). "Politics, Culture, and the Public Sphere: Toward a Postmodern Conception." In *Social Postmodernism: Beyond Identity Politics*, edited by Linda Nicholson and Steven Seidman, 287–314. Cambridge: Cambridge University Press.

50 https://news.bahai.org/story/602/iranian-bahais-sentenced-prison-were-helping-underprivileged-youth

media and cyber operations. I have been subjected to online defamation, hate campaigns, and misinformation circulated through national and international television broadcasts and social media platforms,[51] explicitly targeting both my scholarly work and human rights.[52]

These experiences affirm the theoretical proposition that authoritarian regimes often pathologize non-conformist civic engagement to neutralize its transformative potential (Foucault 1991; Fraser 1995). Acts of community service and educational outreach, especially when enacted by marginalized communities, are perceived not merely as benevolent undertakings but as subversive practices that contest state monopolies over knowledge, development, and authority. Consequently, Bahá'í women's social engagement operates as both a form of epistemic resistance and a site of disciplinary intervention, revealing the deep entanglement of power, gender, and religious difference in Iran's mechanisms of repression.

Social media has become the primary vehicle for disseminating anti-Bahá'í sentiment, with approximately 163,726 posts containing hate speech appearing on government-controlled platforms and websites since 2023.[53] Several online hate campaigns escalated in 2023, primarily orchestrated by state news agencies affiliated with the Islamic Revolutionary Guard Corps (IRGC) and institutions under Khamenei's influence. In July 2023, the IRGC-backed institute Masaf and the Islamic Republic's cyber army launched an online campaign under the hashtag #امیرکبیر_مچکریم, celebrating historical violence against the Bábí and Bahá'í communities and calling for intensified persecution.[54]

The persecution has also extended to economic disenfranchisement and land confiscation. In May 2024, Bahá'í-owned rice paddies in Ahmadabad and Mazandaran provinces were bulldozed by government agents, destroying crops and irrigation systems. These lands, cultivated by Bahá'ís for generations, were seized without legal justification. Similarly, in January 2024, farmlands, rice paddies, and walnut orchards owned by Bahá'í families in

51 Including https://www.youtube.com/watch?v=hTKtUQX42Yo&t=304s, https://www.aparat.com/v/u3b0N, https://www.aparat.com/v/f2089p8

52 A new case was opened in the Attorney General's Office in Tehran, summoning me to court in 2024.

53 These messages are often republished under different titles to reinforce misinformation, with identical content systematically broadcast across multiple sites, an indication of a well-coordinated campaign. High-ranking religious figures, including Supreme Leader Ayatollah Ali Khamenei, have contributed to this effort by issuing decrees that label Bahá'ís as "deviant," "morally corrupt," "misguided," or "unclean." Furthermore, state-driven misinformation campaigns have falsely portrayed Bahá'ís as agents of Israel, foreign spies, and instigators of the September 2022 protests. https://www.bic.org/focus-areas/situation-iranian-bahais/current-situation, https://www.washingtoninstitute.org/policy-analysis/irans-increased-persecution-bahai

54 https://news.bahai.org/story/1519/

Ahmadabad were forcibly confiscated by Iranian officials, who claimed them on behalf of the state.[55]

Another alarming development is the increasing erosion of Bahá'í civil rights, particularly concerning marriage registration and legal recognition. Previously, Bahá'í marriages were documented in physical registries, with notaries issuing marriage certificates. However, the recent transition to an online digital registry system has eliminated the option for registrants to identify as "Bahá'í" or select "other" in the religious affiliation field. Applications that leave this field blank are automatically invalidated, jeopardizing the legal recognition of Bahá'í marriages.[56] This, in turn, affects birth registrations, as children of unregistered marriages are deemed illegitimate under Iranian law – fueling the state's propaganda narrative that Bahá'ís lead immoral lives.

The Iranian state's portrayal of Bahá'ís as existential threats during periods of national crisis operates not as a reactionary impulse but as a calculated mechanism of authoritarian governance. Drawing on Howard Becker's labeling theory, this process of symbolic exclusion redefines Bahá'í identity as inherently subversive, thereby legitimizing systemic repression while deflecting accountability for internal sociopolitical failures (Abdorrahman Boroumand Center and Monash University | Eleos Justice 2024). By constructing Bahá'ís as incompatible with the dominant religious and national identity, the regime deploys a layered strategy of structural, cultural, and direct violence (Galtung 1969). These forms of repression, ranging from economic disenfranchisement to judicial persecution, are increasingly veiled in legalistic discourses that contradict both the Iranian constitution and international human rights norms.

This framing is particularly salient in the disproportionate targeting of Bahá'í women, whose social contributions and moral leadership are recast as ideological transgressions. Their persecution reflects what scholars of authoritarian resilience identify as selective repression used to suppress alternative ethical frameworks and sustain hegemonic control. Religious intolerance thus becomes a political technology of exclusion, foreclosing pluralism and constraining democratic possibility. This analysis sharpens existing scholarship by showing how gendered religious repression simultaneously reinforces authoritarian power and generates new forms of epistemic agency. Yet the growing visibility of these injustices, within Iran and internationally, signals fissures in the regime's narrative authority.

55 https://news.bahai.org/story/1608/, https://iranfocus.com/general/51277-iranian-regime-agents-destroy-bahai-farms/, https://www.bic.org/news/iranian-government-destroys-bahai-owned-farmlands-latest-cruel-example-economic-apartheid

56 This issue becomes even more discriminatory when a Bahá'í and a Muslim wish to marry. According to Bahá'í law, two marriage ceremonies are required – one in the Bahá'í tradition and another in the Islamic tradition. The situation becomes even more complex and exclusive when a Bahá'í woman seeks to marry a Muslim man, as the intersection of her gender and religious identity further amplifies the challenges and restrictions she faces.

Two Bahá'í Women Known as Icons of Resilience in Iran

In this section, I examine the cases of two Bahá'í women among the many subjected to arrest, detention, and imprisonment. They are selected for the distinct and sustained nature of their experiences over the past 13 years, which offer critical insight into broader patterns of repression. My long-standing engagement with these women since 2001 in educational and community-building endeavors provides a contextualized understanding of their resilience and lived experiences. Following their release in 2017, I met with both and conducted an in-depth interview with Mahvash in 2021. Later, I invited her to speak online in my gender and religion course at the University of Oslo in the same year. As direct access to Fariba was not possible, this chapter draws on a multi-method qualitative approach, combining interview data, digital ethnography, and secondary analysis. It incorporates publicly available social media posts shared by close relatives, alongside other reliable digital sources. Although permission to use these materials was obtained, all social media content has been anonymized and paraphrased, with identifying details removed to protect individuals and their families living under conditions of political repression.

In December 2022, the BIC issued a public statement highlighting the escalating repression and violence perpetrated by Iranian authorities against their own citizens.[57] The statement specifically addressed the case of two prominent Bahá'í women, Mahvash Sabet Shahriyari and Fariba Kamalabadi, who, after enduring a decade of imprisonment, were sentenced to an additional ten years in prison. Widely regarded as symbols of resilience within Iran, their re-arrest on 31 July 2022 marked the beginning of a renewed wave of persecution targeting the Bahá'í community[58] (Bahá'í International Community 2022). The latest prison sentence was issued following a one-hour trial on 21 November, during which the majority of the proceedings were dominated by the judge's insults and humiliation of the defendants. This trial took place nearly four months after their arrest. Judge Iman Afshari, presiding over Branch 26 of the Revolutionary Court in Tehran, reprimanded the two women, stating that they had "not learned their lesson" from their previous imprisonment.[59] Their story is one of resilience amidst the harshest of conditions.

57 https://www.bic.org/news/unbelievable-injustice-mahvash-sabet-and-fariba-kamalabadi-sentenced-second-decade-prison-iran

58 Since their detention, over 320 Bahá'ís have faced various forms of persecution, including arbitrary arrests, home demolitions, and intensified state-sponsored propaganda campaigns (Bahá'í International Community 2022). Dozens of Bahá'ís have been detained across different regions, including Shiraz and Mazandaran province, while homes belonging to Bahá'ís in the village of Roshankouh were systematically destroyed. https://news.bahai.org/story/1608/

59 https://www.bic.org/news/unbelievable-injustice-mahvash-sabet-and-fariba-kamalabadi-sentenced-second-decade-prison-iran

Mahvash Sabet Shahriyari

Mahvash Sabet Shahriyari,[60] a prominent educator, was arrested on 31 July 2022, when security forces raided her home in Tehran. During the arrest, it was reported that her kneecaps were broken during the interrogation. A few months later, in November 2022, it was revealed that she had been charged with "founding or leading an organization that aims to disrupt national security" (Article 498 of the Islamic Penal Code). In December 2022, Mahvash was sentenced to ten years in prison following a one-hour trial held on 21 November 2022. The charges stemmed from her role as a leader in the Bahá'í community and her long-standing dedication to education, particularly for marginalized Bahá'í youth.

By August 2023, the Tehran Court of Appeal upheld her sentence. Throughout this period, it was reported that Mahvash, who had been diagnosed with multiple illnesses, had been hospitalized several times. Despite her worsening health, prison authorities failed to provide adequate medical care. In October 2024, it became clear that her respiratory and lung conditions were severe, yet she was denied proper treatment. A month later, in December 2024, her worsening cardiac condition forced her transfer to Rajaei Hospital in Tehran for emergency care.[61]

Mahvash, now 72 years old,[62] has devoted much of her life to education, particularly for those systematically excluded from mainstream institutions. Dismissed from public education due to her Bahá'í Faith, she had a distinguished career as a teacher, school principal, and collaborator with Iran's National Literacy Committee, dedicating herself to expanding educational opportunities.[63]

60 Born on 4 February 1953 in Ardestan, Mahvash moved to Tehran in her childhood. She pursued psychology in university, earning a bachelor's degree before beginning her career as an educator. In 1973, she married Siyvash Sabet, and together they raised a son and a daughter.

61 https://www.uscirf.gov/religious-prisoners-conscience/forb-victims-database/mahvash-sabet

62 In my interview with Mahvash, she recounted a lifetime of exclusion and discrimination, describing what it meant to grow up as an "other" in Iranian society. She recalled her early school days: "When I started school, boys and girls walked together, but older boys threw stones at Bahá'í children and called us names. I complained to my mother, but she told me to be patient, to pray for them, and to stay strong. She taught me to be an agent of change, not a victim." But discrimination was not just from students. One day, after being falsely accused by classmates, she was severely beaten by the school principal. "She whipped me with pomegranate branches soaked in water until my hands bled. Then she expelled me." For six months, Mahvash suffered from infections and fever. Eventually, her parents took her to a hospital in Tehran for serious treatment. Despite her father's complaint to the police, nothing changed when she returned to school.

63 She explained, "When I was 20, I found my soulmate. At that time, I was a university student and also working as a schoolteacher. When my son turned three, the Islamic Revolution came and drastically altered our lives. I was expelled from university because I was a Bahá'í, and I was fired from my teaching job by the school principal. My dismissal form explicitly stated that I was a follower of the 'deviant Bahá'í sect.' I firmly believe that the Bahá'í Faith represents divine truth and is not some cult or deviant sect. However, this is how it was labeled by the supreme leader of the Islamic Republic of Iran, and as a result, Bahá'ís are denied basic rights under Iranian law. The Iranian constitution, based on Sharia law, does not even recognize Bahá'ís as a religious minority."

For 15 years, prior to her first arrest in 2008, Mahvash led the Bahá'í Institute for Higher Education (BIHE),[64] an institution that provided an alternative to the state-controlled education system, which discriminated against Bahá'í youth. Reflecting on this experience in an interview, she explained as follows:

> Just a few years after the Islamic revolution, the Bahá'ís decided to develop their own strategies in response to their persecution by the Islamic government: constructive resilience,[65] a strategy in which the persecuted do not seek reprisal but rather peace, prosperity in their own pursuits in the context of an overweening commitment to a vision of unity for all mankind. It has been a learning process, but I feel sure that, in future, history will draw many lessons from the response of the Bahá'í community of Iran.
>
> A few of us had the vision of creating an opportunity for the Bahá'í students, all of whom are deprived of higher education by the state. At the time, my daughter was two and a half. Working systematically, we established an unofficial university that is now recognized by many universities around the world, and many Bahá'í students who have graduated from this institution have gone on to pursue graduate work in other countries. However, the Islamic government has resisted this effort, repeatedly arresting professors and students of this institution for teaching or studying in it. For nineteen years, I was a member of the academic board of this institution to which the professors give their time without remuneration and which is tuition-free.[66]

Her first arrest on 5 March 2008 marked a turning point in her life. Recalling that day, she described the moment as follows:

> It was at my daughter's wedding celebration that, for the second time, Islamic security guards attacked my home and I was arrested. My daughter

64 The Bahá'í Institute for Higher Education (BIHE) was founded in 1987 in response to the Iranian government's denial of higher education to Bahá'í students. Offering 56 university-level programs across five faculties, Sciences, Engineering, Business and Management, Humanities, and Social Sciences, BIHE has maintained high academic standards despite facing government opposition. Its graduates have excelled internationally, reflecting the institution's commitment to academic excellence, innovation, and resilience. BIHE remains a symbol of the Bahá'í community's dedication to education and the belief that access to knowledge is a fundamental human right. https://www.bihe.org/

65 The concept of *constructive resilience* was introduced by Michael Karlberg in his 2010 scholarly article, "Constructive Resilience: The Bahá'í Response to Oppression." published in *Peace & Change* (35, no. 2: 222–257. https://doi.org/10.1111/j.1468-0130.2009.00627.x). Since its publication, this framework has become a central part of Bahá'í community discourse, providing a conceptual lens to articulate the Iranian Bahá'í community's sustained and principled response to long-standing systemic discrimination.

66 *Elixir Journal* (Sabet Sarvestany, Issue 13, https://elixir-journal.org/issue13/interview2.php).

> was still getting her hair done and, and everyone was waiting for her to come in with her white dress. I had to step out for a minute to do some last-minute arrangements. When the Islamic security guards burst into our home, my husband promised them that I would report to their office the next day, but they insisted that I should come the moment I got home. When I was released thirty-four days later, my daughter was still crying.[67]

In her second arrest while other members of the Bahá'í administrative group known as the "Friends"[68] were arrested in Tehran, Mahvash was detained in Mashhad. She had been summoned under the pretext of needing to answer questions related to the burial of an individual in the Bahá'í cemetery in Mashhad.[69] Mahvash shared her harrowing experience:

> I was held in solitary confinement for more than six months, subjected to torture and interrogation. The government agents asked me to spy on the Bahá'í community. They threatened and tried to lure me into complying with their unreasonable and immoral demands. They also tried to enter into ideological discussions with me. When they saw that my colleagues and I would not accept their demands, they charged us with serious crimes grounded in baseless accusations so that they could execute us.
>
> They leveled charges such as spying for hostile states or "corruption on earth," or acting against national security and against the government, but they did not have a single shred of evidence to prove these allegations. Some well-known lawyers such as Shirin Ebadi, the only Iranian woman who was awarded the Nobel Peace Prize, for her efforts for democracy and human rights in Iran, agreed to represent us and defend our case; however, the investigating judge issued an indictment against us, requesting the death sentence.
>
> After two and a half years in solitary confinement, waiting daily for the sentence of execution to be carried out, we were transported to another public prison outside Tehran and given a sentence of twenty years in prison. During the two and a half years of my confinement, I was with another woman who was my colleague and dear friend. Fariba and I were imprisoned with other "social criminals" in a public prison for women.

67 *Elixir Journal* (Sabet Sarvestany, Issue 13, https://elixir-journal.org/issue13/interview2.php).

68 The Bahá'í 7, also known as the "Yaran" (friends), were seven Iranian Bahá'í community leaders arrested in 2008 who served ten-year prison sentences in Iran. They were responsible for the social, cultural, and religious affairs of the Bahá'í community in Iran. The seven prisoners of conscience were Mahvash Sabet, Fariba Kamalabadi, Jamaloddin Khanjani, Afif Naeimi, Saeid Rezaie, Behrouz Tavakkoli, and Vahid Tizfahm. https://news.bahai.org/human-rights/iran/yaran-special-report/profiles

69 https://www.bic.org/mrs-mahvash-sabet

> This was done to humiliate us,[70] but in fact we seized the opportunity to create a friendly environment in the prison, so we could educate and serve these disadvantaged women. However, before long, the prison intelligence officials asked the other prisoners to stay away from us. They told the women that we were being kind to them because we wanted to convert them. Then the prison intelligence officials deported us to a prison filled with thugs, who were very dangerous.[71]

When I asked her, "How do you feel now that you are a free woman, someone who has conquered extreme discrimination and injustice? How do you practice 'constructive resilience' in your own life now?" she responded as follows:

> I should say that the spirit of Iranian society was totally changed by the time I was released. So many well-known people in Iran, from different walks of life and in pursuit of different causes, wished to visit me. For seven months, we welcomed to our home intellectuals, social and political activists, even the family members of clergy and those in high level governmental and non-governmental positions. Most of them offered an apology for what the Islamic government has done to the Bahá'ís of Iran. It was one of the lessons I learned – how much time I needed and what I did in those last ten years to achieve such success. I believe that my imprisonment, and all the discrimination and injustice that went along with it, were part of this victory. I believe that because of the injustices of the last forty-two years, all eighty-five million of the people in Iran know truth about the Bahá'í Faith.
>
> Just one week after my release, without any justification, the Islamic government confiscated our house and any property that remained after the revolution. Still, Bahá'ís are arrested, imprisoned for years, their shops are closed and their properties and houses are confiscated. Just a few weeks ago, all the lands of Bahá'í farmers in one of the villages in the north of Iran were confiscated and their houses destroyed. Not a single article of Iranian law is designed to defend the civil rights of Bahá'ís.
>
> All my life, I have borne witness to a historical genocide, but I myself am still alive, full of energy and full of ideas. I am still editing and publishing the poems I wrote in prison. My poems in prison were my voice

70 Mahvash explained that: "After eight and a half years, our sentence of twenty years was, they said, found to be invalid, based on some obscure legal article, but, in fact, it was the pressure of public opinion across the world, I believe, that brought the change, and our sentence was shortened to ten years. On the day of my release, my fellow prisoners were so happy, they held a feast for me, distributed sweets, sang freedom songs and danced! I humbly bowed before them in respect for their courage and resistance."

71 *Elixir Journal* (Sabet Sarvestany, Issue 13, https://elixir-journal.org/issue13/interview2.php).

when the Islamic government closed all the doors and deprived me of the opportunity to serve others. My poems were the voice of a captured bird who sang of peace, unity, love, truth, and prosperity of all humanity, in order to bring light into the darkness. My poems are the voice of my faith.

The first volume of my poems was translated into English and published as Prison Poems in the UK, when I was still in prison. The book won the World Writers' Association Award for Brave Writers in 2017. In 2019, it also won the Words Award at the Fredrikstad Literary Festival in Norway. This work has been translated into five other languages – French, German, Italian, Norwegian and Spanish – and it has been published in Persian in Spain. The second volume of my prison poems, entitled Freedom, is also being published, and the third volume, entitled A Love Story, has recently been published in Norway. The fourth and fifth volumes of these poems will be ready for publication soon.[72]

On 20 November 2023 during her third imprisonment, Mahvash wrote a heartfelt letter from her cell, calling for empathy and understanding. Her words resonated as a poignant call for her fellow Iranians to listen to the experiences of the Bahá'í community and recognize their right to a dignified life, free from persecution. In a letter widely circulated on social media, she urged Iranians not to follow the government's lead in ostracizing Bahá'ís, the country's most persecuted religious minority. Mahvash implored as follows:

> If the [Iranian] government has ostracized the Bahá'ís, please do not follow their lead. . . . We, like everyone else, have the right to a decent life, to enjoy citizenship rights, to pursue suitable employment according to our abilities, to attend university . . . and to use our full potential for the development of the country.[73]

In her letter she recalled the personal toll of the revolution: "My father, my brothers, all my relatives, friends, and colleagues gradually became unemployed and homeless, and our life was thrown into turmoil." For Mahvash, it was not just a loss of livelihood, but the loss of identity, a feeling of being rendered an "other" in her own country. In another part, Mahvash highlighted the continued suffering of the Bahá'í community, drawing attention to the numerous arrests, confiscations, and executions that had defined their experience.

72 Conducted by the author in early 2021 via Skype across multiple sessions, this interview forms part of a longer, in-depth conversation. Excerpts cited here are drawn from this fieldwork, published in *Elixir Journal* (Sabet Sarvestany, Issue 13, https://elixir-journal.org/issue13/interview2.php).

73 The full letter is accessible at the following link. https://iranwire.com/en/bahais-of-iran/122701-my-story-is-yours-bahai-woman-writes-to-iranians-from-evin-prison/

"It was as if all of us, the Bahá'ís, were instantaneously ostracized. Suddenly, my country and my heritage were stripped away." Mahvash's letter took a painful turn when she recounted the time when she was released in 2017, after serving ten years for her faith. "No one came to welcome me on the day of my freedom," she recalled. "My family was expecting my release a day later. But they were not allowed to call me . . . I was released from prison without any family waiting for me, without money, and even without an address to go to."

Later in her letter she mentioned about her third arrest: "I spent 42 days in solitary confinement. It was a form of torture, physical abuse, insults, threats, and slander. My COVID symptoms were severe,[74] and I was hospitalized three times." Mahvash's third imprisonment was marked by the same unjust treatment, as she was charged with "organizing a group under a deviant sect with the aim of disrupting the security of the country." She vehemently denied these accusations, asserting that no evidence was presented against her. "The prosecutor, the investigator, nor the judge could produce a single document to support their claims," she wrote. In her letter, Mahvash reflected on a chilling conversation with an interrogator from years ago, who told her, "Yes, but we shall determine whether it is horizontal or vertical," a haunting reference to whether she would leave the prison dead or alive. Now, from her cell, Mahvash expresses her disillusionment with the justice system and the government, stating, "I have lost faith in justice from the government. Compatriots! My story is yours. Please do not ostracize me. Listen to our narratives in our own words."[75]

Fariba Kamalabadi

The second woman who was arrested alongside Mahvash was Mrs. Fariba Kamalabadi,[76] born on 12 September 1962 in Tehran. She was an outstanding student, graduating from high school with honors, but was subsequently denied access to higher education due to her Bahá'í Faith. However, despite her academic ability, her dreams of pursuing higher education were dashed by the Iranian government's policy of discrimination against the Bahá'í community. Undeterred by this setback, Fariba embarked on an unconventional educational journey in her mid-thirties. She spent eight years engaged in informal

74 When Mahvash was arrested on 31 July 2022, while visiting her sister in Ramsar. At the time, Mahvash and her husband were recovering from severe COVID-19 symptoms, but despite her health condition, she was detained and transferred to solitary confinement in the infamous Ward 209 of Evin Prison, known for holding political prisoners and those arrested for their beliefs.

75 The full letter is accessible at the following link: https://iranwire.com/en/bahais-of-iran/122701-my-story-is-yours-bahai-woman-writes-to-iranians-from-evin-prison/

76 In 1982, Fariba married Ruhollah Taefi, a fellow Bahá'í, and together they had three children. The youngest of their children was only 13 years old when Mrs. Kamalabadi was arrested in 2008, an event that would change her family's life forever. https://www.bic.org/mrs-fariba-kamalabadi

study, determined to pursue knowledge despite the systemic barriers in her way. Her perseverance led her to the BIHE; there, she earned an advanced degree in psychology.

Her experience of persecution, however, was not limited to her own arrest. It began long before, with the suffering of her father. In the 1980s, when she was still a young woman, her father, a physician, was dismissed from his position in the government health service because of his Bahá'í Faith. This was only the beginning of his ordeal. Her father was later imprisoned and subjected to torture, a brutal reflection of the systemic repression faced by the Bahá'í community in Iran. The persecution that Fariba and her family endured, from the loss of opportunities to the unjust suffering of her father, became the backdrop of her own story, one of resilience and a steadfast commitment to her faith and principles. On 31 July 2022 security forces arrested Fariba in Tehran after raiding her home. In December 2022, she was sentenced to ten years in prison following a one-hour trial on 21 November 2022. In August 2023, the Tehran Court of Appeal upheld her sentence, with Kamalabadi facing charges of "forming and leading groups to act against national security."[77] It was the second time she received a ten-year sentence, following her release from Evin Prison in 2017.[78]

Even as she faced arrest and imprisonment, she never wavered in her belief in the right to education, justice, and dignity for all people, regardless of their religious background. An anonymous family source who documented the family's experiences through social media described several incidents following Fariba's second arrest.[79] The source recounted that family members were occasionally permitted only brief encounters with Fariba during legal proceedings, during which she reportedly expressed sorrow at being unable to fulfil her role as a mother while also describing her efforts to care for and support younger women detained alongside her. The same source further reported repeated occasions when prison authorities initially approved family visits but withdrew permission shortly before the scheduled meeting. These sudden cancellations caused considerable emotional distress for family members, particularly children, highlighting how restrictions on family contact functioned not only to isolate political prisoners but also as a form of psychological pressure on their loved ones.

The same family source also reflected on the close relationship between Fariba and her grandchildren, illustrating the intergenerational impact of repeated imprisonment. According to the account, one granddaughter had been too young to remember Fariba's previous imprisonment, but during the second period of incarceration she was old enough to understand her grandmother's

77 https://www.uscirf.gov/religious-prisoners-conscience/forb-victims-database/fariba-kamalabadi

78 https://bahaipedia.org/Fariba_Kamalabadi

79 Anonymous family source, archived social media material in the author's possession.

prolonged absence. On one occasion, the child innocently asked whether her grandmother could leave prison to attend her birthday. After learning that this was impossible, she quietly withdrew,[80] revealing the emotional burden that political imprisonment placed on children who struggled to make sense of a loved one's absence through the logic of everyday family life. This account demonstrates how the consequences of imprisonment extended beyond the incarcerated individual to shape the emotional worlds of younger generations.

The family source further reflected on the profound emotional consequences of Fariba's repeated imprisonment across generations. The account illustrates how prolonged incarceration reshaped the family's experience of time, with years marked not by ordinary milestones but by cycles of arrest, imprisonment, and release. Fariba was absent from many of the most significant moments in her daughter's life, including her graduation, engagement, marriage, pregnancy, and the birth of her first child. Both mother and daughter were deprived of irreplaceable experiences that would ordinarily have strengthened their relationship. These repeated separations fractured the rhythms of family life, yet the enduring emotional bond between them demonstrates the resilience of familial relationships despite sustained state repression.

The source also reflected on the experiences of Fariba's grandchildren, observing that one granddaughter would spend much of her childhood separated from her grandmother before they could eventually be reunited. Rather than representing the passage of time alone, these years symbolize the cumulative impact of political persecution on successive generations. The account recalled two symbolic family memories: one in which Fariba, while imprisoned, prepared a modest birthday gift for her granddaughter, and another recalling an earlier imprisonment when she had cultivated a single carrot as a birthday present for her teenage daughter. Although separated by decades, these acts of care illustrate Fariba's determination to preserve family relationships through small but deeply meaningful expressions of affection. They reveal how caregiving, love, and maternal commitment became everyday forms of resilience in the face of prolonged imprisonment and the systematic persecution of the Bahá'í community.

Beyond this individual family's experience, an analysis of publicly available Twitter and Instagram posts published between June 2023 and June 2024 reveals a growing sense of solidarity between those inside and outside prison. Across multiple social media accounts, imprisoned activists and their families documented how acts of resistance, mutual support, and shared experiences transcended prison walls. The resilience of incarcerated individuals appeared to inspire wider Iranian society, while prisoners themselves drew strength

80 Information derived from anonymized social media posts shared by a family member. The material has been paraphrased, and identifying details have been removed to protect the individual and their family.

from the activism taking place beyond prison. This reciprocal relationship illustrates the emergence of a shared community of resistance linking those in detention with supporters outside prison. One anonymized family account, for example, described a telephone conversation in which Fariba recounted a gathering among imprisoned women where participants shared their personal experiences in order to recognize that, despite their different backgrounds and circumstances, they were united by a common struggle.[81] This account illustrates how collective storytelling became an important source of solidarity, hope, and resilience among political prisoners.

During a telephone conversation, Fariba described a gathering among imprisoned women where participants shared their personal experiences, emphasizing that their struggles formed part of a common story. This referred to the global **#OurStoryIsOne**[82] campaign, launched by the international Bahá'í community to commemorate the 40th anniversary of the execution of ten Bahá'í women in Shiraz during the 1980s.[83] While the campaign was taking place worldwide, Fariba recreated its spirit inside the prison, transforming a global act of remembrance into a shared space of solidarity, resilience, and collective resistance among her fellow inmates.

Simin Fahandej (2023), the BIC representative to the United Nations in Geneva, reflects on the significance of this solidarity:

> We are deeply moved by the level of support already seen for the campaign. The response highlights the shared struggle for gender equality in Iran and the interconnectedness of our stories. The resilience of Iranian women today is part of the same narrative of resistance that the ten Bahá'í women of Shiraz embodied four decades ago.

She further emphasizes,

> The blood, tears, and sacrifices of thousands of young women in Iran today seeking equality echo the injustice suffered by these ten women. Their tragic deaths became a symbol of resilience, a chapter in the ongoing struggle for justice and gender equality in Iran.[84]

81 Several accounts in these pages draw on publicly available social media posts shared by close relatives. Although permission to use these materials was obtained, all sources have been anonymized and paraphrased, and identifying details have been removed to protect individuals and their families.

82 https://news.bahai.org/story/1674/

83 This campaign honors the ten Bahá'í women who, in the face of persecution, upheld their faith and principles of oneness, equality, and justice, even at the cost of their lives. The movement has garnered widespread support, manifesting in various forms of artistic expression, including songs, paintings, poems, graphic art, craftwork, and written tributes from public figures.

84 https://news.bahai.org/story/1674/

In this regard I personally also organized three events in Finland, both within academic settings and for the public, in connection with this campaign. These events were not only intellectually stimulating but also deeply impactful. For the first time, women from diverse backgrounds, ranging from students to the mayor of city, as well as representatives from universities and NGOs, came together to share their experiences of discrimination. Their narratives reflected how factors such as religion, nationality, ethnicity, gender, and political views shaped their encounters with exclusion and inequality. My motivation for organizing these events was deeply personal. One of the ten Bahá'í women executed in Shiraz was my aunt,[85] and as a Bahá'í woman, activist, and Scholar at Risk,[86] I have also experienced systemic discrimination and exclusion. Beyond personal connection, what compelled this analysis is the recognition that, following the WLF uprisings, mechanisms of persecution once directed at minorities have expanded to target all those advocating equality and justice, spreading across society and systematically silencing dissent.

Although no official record exists of events following the gathering Fariba described, where women shared their experiences, evidence from related incidents, such as brief hunger strikes by political prisoners in solidarity with Bahá'í inmates, and vice versa, points to a sustained culture of mutual support. These accounts of solidarity and collective resistance suggest that such gatherings were crucial in fostering connection among imprisoned women and reinforcing their epistemic agency under conditions of systemic oppression. On 13 November 2023, an anonymous family source shared a prison letter from Fariba addressing the Iranian people amid intensified persecution of the Bahá'í community. The letter testifies to systemic injustice while underscoring the resilience and courage of Bahá'í women, exemplified by her decision to write despite known risks. Fariba began her letter with the following:

> On the morning of November 7, in a phone call with my husband, I found the opportunity to talk with my son-in-law's mother, Mrs. Shoghangiz Sorourian, who had travelled from Hamadan to Tehran for medical treatment and to visit her daughter. I heard from her that a group of security agents had attacked their house in Hamadan, had broken down the door, and had looted it in the absence of the owner.
>
> My mind immediately returned to 1987. To the time when Mrs. Shoghangiz and her husband were arrested for being Bahá'ís and transferred from Hamadan to Evin Prison in Tehran.
>
> At that time, they had three young children aged 4, 6, and 8, who were deprived of parental care due to the arrest of their parents. After several months of not hearing from each other, for a long time the relatives took

85 https://www.iranrights.org/memorial/story/-3257/akhtar-sabet-sarvestani,
86 https://www.scholarsatrisk.org/annual-report-2021/

all three children to Tehran every week to meet their father on one day and their mother on the other day, in prison, and then return to Hamadan and school.

It goes without saying that arresting parents with young children is a deliberate act and that, regrettably, it continues still and leaves irreparable negative effects on children and their parents.

It is an example of "child torture."

That same 4-year-old girl grew into a young woman. In the late 80s, she was arrested in Hamadan and jailed in to Nahavand Prison. Then it was the turn of her elderly and lonely mother to go from Hamadan to Nahavand, every week, to visit her young daughter in the general ward of Nahavand Prison, in very inappropriate conditions.

Now, after about 36 years, the house of this 82-year-old lady has been brutally attacked and looted, and her mental security has been deliberately disturbed. I also heard that the house of Mrs. Akhtar Kosari (Naiemi), who is 88 years old and has Alzheimer's, has been also attacked and ransacked.

She is the wife of Dr. Firouz Naiemi, a prominent, well-known and popular medical specialist in Hamadan, who was brutally arrested along with six other Bahá'ís at the beginning of the 1979 revolution and was executed as a result of terrible torture.

The other two houses that were attacked were the houses of Mrs. Pouran Habibi (Khandel) and her son Mehran Khandel. Her husband, Mr. Hosein Khandel, and her two uncles, Mr. Soheil and Mr. Sohrab Habibi, were among the same seven people who were executed.

My Wednesday morning started with this news and with thinking about the sad 40-year history of this family. My heart was full of sadness. Sadness for the severity of oppression and sadness for the severity of the government's hostility towards a group of the most peaceful and law-abiding Iranian citizens.

The continuation of the same sadness that had taken over my heart, and the hearts of many of my dear compatriots since the end of last summer following the people's protest uprising against the death of Mahsa (Gina) Amini and the death of many dear Iranian youth in the course of pursuing their basic human rights.

In the afternoon of the same day, I had the opportunity to call my children for a few minutes, when I heard the attack on Bahá'í homes was not limited to those few families. In fact, about 25 houses were attacked and ransacked and nine people were arrested and imprisoned i n Hamadan. I also heard about the arrest of about six other Bahá'ís in Karaj. One of them is the nephew of my husband, Foad Taefi, who has three young and teenage children.

During his childhood, Foad also witnessed his father's imprisonment and later his mother's arrest in Mashhad, and then his father-in-law's arrest and imprisonment in Rajai Shahr Prison in Karaj. Among those who were arrested in Karaj are a young couple who also have two young children. It can be safely said that there is not a single Bahá'í family in Iran that does not have a past full of suffering and injuries like these in several successive generations.

After hearing this terrible news, I remembered a time in August 2022, during my interrogation sessions, when I was explained to the interrogator:

> "You know the Bahá'í group that was responsible for managing the internal affairs of the Bahá'ís has been closed since 2008, when I was in prison. After my release in 2017, I have been under surveillance every moment, and you know that the accusation of 'forming an illegal group' is not true. And now I, like all Bahá'ís living in Iran, have no administrative responsibility. So what is the reason for repeating this accusation?"

The investigator replied:

> "Yes, we know that you didn't have any responsibility during this time, but in our opinion, all Bahá'ís who have remained in Iran and have not left Iran ought to be arrest ed and imprisoned. If we could, we would imprison all of them."

At that moment, I thought this answer was the only justification for my illegal arrest; but now, by attacking the houses of some elderly women, I am sure that, on that day, he was talking about an objective and real strategy of the government regarding the Bahá'í community in Iran.

"All the Bahá'ís who have stayed in Iran and have not left Iran deserve to be arrested and imprisoned."

I am writing these lines, with a sad heart, to my dear grandchildren Nava and Diba, one of whose grandmothers is spending her twelfth year of imprisonment in Evin Prison, under such unfortunate conditions, while the other grandmother is 82 years old and, after enduring prison with her husband and away from three young children 36 years ago, is now deprived of even the basic right to live safely in her home.

And for dear Sina, Faran and Fares Taefi, who have seen and heard the imprisonment of their father, two grandfathers, and their uncle. And for all the children of Iran and the justice-loving people of my beloved land, who have lost their loved ones and young people due to cruelty. Because "our story is one." Maybe hearing these painful but true stories will make us try harder, so that justice replaces injustice and light replaces darkness.[87]

87 The original letter is in Perisan. https://iranbahaipersecution.bic.org/index.php/archive/fariba-kamalabadis-letter-inside-evin-prison-reaction-rising-attacks-countrys-bahai

Letter-writing by prisoners of conscience and political detainees constitutes a significant form of resistance and agency.[88] In the aftermath of the WLF movement, these letters have circulated widely through social media and in translation, amplifying prisoners' voices and documenting conditions of confinement. This circulation has, in turn, mobilized the Iranian diaspora, facilitating transnational advocacy that foregrounds individual cases and exerts pressure on foreign governments to hold the Iranian state accountable and secure the release of detainees.[89]

The letters of Fariba and Mahvash extend beyond personal testimony, offering a critical lens on the systemic persecution of religious minorities in Iran. They reveal enduring patterns of state repression, such as arbitrary arrest, property raids, and psychological intimidation, that reflect the criminalization of identity and the maintenance of hegemonic control. Through the construction of Bahá'ís as internal enemies, these narratives expose both the intergenerational and gendered dimensions of persecution. While situated within Iran's specific context, they resonate with broader patterns of minority oppression. At the same time, these letters enact epistemic and political agency, reclaiming dignity, memory, and collective resistance.

On 9 December 2023 the same family source wrote that "Fariba and Mahvash have announced a three-day hunger strike on December 9, 10, and 11 in protest against the government's destructive policies. They demand the recognition of the civil rights of Bahá'ís in Iran." This event marked a significant moment in the history of Bahá'í persecution, as it was the first time that Bahá'í individuals had publicly announced a hunger strike in response to the Bahá'í community unjust persecution. The hunger strike both shocked and garnered admiration from Iranian society and the international Bahá'í community, illustrating the depth of the Iranian Bahá'í women's resilience. Notably, the protest extended beyond the prison walls, some Bahá'ís not incarcerated also declared their intention to join the hunger strike,[90] showing solidarity with Fariba and Mahvash. Inside the prison, several other women joined in solidarity, further amplifying the collective voice of resistance.[91]

The solidarity exhibited among women within Iranian prisons illustrates what scholars such as Fraser (1995) and Mohanty (2003) identify as counter-public formation: a space where marginalized actors, through shared

88 Letters by Varisheh Moradi, Pakhshan Azizi, Narges Mohamadi, and Sepideh Gholian are prominent examples of this form of resistance.

89 Online networks such as the Global Network for Woman, Life, Freedom and the Global Campaign to Stop Executions in Iran, along with initiatives like "Voice of Prisoners" and "Voice of Revolution," exemplify transnational forms of activism that connect Iranians inside and outside the country. These networks play a crucial role in amplifying the voices of prisoners and mobilizing global advocacy, particularly in efforts to halt executions in Iran.

90 [@OAfaghi]. (2023, Dec 9) and [@jenabeishan]. (2023, Dec 9).

91 [@golrokhiraee]. (2023, Dec 9).

vulnerability and mutual care, construct alternative modes of political belonging. This carceral solidarity transcended ethnic, religious, and ideological boundaries, forging affective alliances that serve as the foundation for broader resistance beyond prison walls. These dynamics were mirrored in the Iranian diaspora, where rapid mobilization reflected what Sidney Tarrow (1998) refers to as transnational activism, movements that, although rooted in domestic grievances, gain traction and sustainability through global networks of support. Through digital campaigns, public demonstrations, academic forums, and cultural events across Europe, North America, and Australia, diasporic communities have amplified the voices of those subjected to state violence in Iran. Social media platforms such as Instagram and Twitter function as spaces of discursive resistance, reshaping the narrative of the uprising for international audiences, while universities and civil society actors contribute through panels, conferences, and exhibitions. Drawing from my participation in these initiatives, academic and non-academic, I have observed an unprecedented convergence of actors committed to justice, gender equality, and pluralism. This wave of activism has been notably inclusive, engaging individuals across ideological, generational, and professional divides. From a theoretical perspective, this reflects the emergence of what Keck and Sikkink (1998) term "advocacy networks," coalitions united not by homogeneous ideology, but by shared ethical commitments to human rights and democratic reform. However, consistent with observations from social movement theory (Della Porta and Diani 2006), internal frictions have surfaced. Disagreements over political affiliation, representational legitimacy, and discursive authority have occasionally fragmented these coalitions, highlighting the difficulty of maintaining cohesion within decentralized grassroots movements. Such tensions, while not inherently detrimental, reveal the contested nature of collective identity formation in exile, where divergent historical experiences and visions for Iran's future intersect.

One emerging pattern within this landscape has been the proliferation of "activist identity" among individuals previously unengaged in political life. This shift reflects a broader cultural transformation and a redefinition of civic responsibility. Yet it also raises concerns about the commodification of dissent. What appears as political engagement may, in some instances, resemble what Sara Ahmed (2012) calls "performative activism," acts that seek visibility or partisan validation rather than fostering inclusive solidarity. When activism centers on amplifying factional voices at the expense of marginalized perspectives, it risks replicating the very exclusions it seeks to redress. In contrast, genuine civic resistance is grounded in a commitment to relational ethics and the amplification of silenced narratives. This moment thus signifies not only a rupture in authoritarian discourse but also a critical test of whether oppositional movements can meaningfully embody the democratic values they claim to uphold. As observed in the aftermath of the WLF movement, this challenge has exposed underlying tensions, rendering solidarities increasingly fragile and susceptible to fragmentation.

Returning to the focus of this chapter, between September 2022 and spring 2025, the Islamic Republic of Iran has followed a paradoxical trajectory: while intensifying authoritarian repression in response to widespread unrest, grassroots resistance, particularly among Iranian women, has become more visible, diverse, and globally resonant. Central to this dynamic are Mahvash Sabet and Fariba Kamalabadi, two imprisoned members of the unrecognized religious minority in Iran, whose open letters and joint hunger strike in December 2023 constitute powerful acts of civil resistance. Their interventions not only contest the regime's silencing of dissent but also foreground the enduring resilience and embodied agency of women under systemic oppression.

Their imprisonment reveals both the targeted repression of the Bahá'í community and the gendered dynamics of incarceration, positioning Bahá'í women as symbols of intergenerational resistance (Bahá'í International Community 2023). Their experiences demonstrate the intersection of religious and gender-based persecution, generating forms of spiritual, relational, and epistemic resistance. Through caregiving, narrative, and symbolic resilience, Mahvash and Fariba enact intersectional nonviolent resistance, countering punitive state logic with ethics of solidarity and moral clarity. Marked by family separation and ideological coercion, their stories underscore the role of memory and narrative as practices of political survival, redefining the resistance of minority and marginalized people in ways that challenge authoritarian power.

Conclusion

In this chapter, I have argued that the epistemic, ethical, and embodied agency of persecuted Iranian women, exemplified through the experiences of Bahá'í women, constitutes a transformative force within broader struggles for justice, gender equality, and democratic expression among marginalized communities. Their faith-based practices, moral commitments, and narrative strategies disrupt the state's ideological monopoly by asserting alternative visions of dignity, solidarity, and collective flourishing. By situating these forms of agency within the sociopolitical context shaped by the WLF movement, the analysis demonstrates how minority women convert personal resilience into constructive and pluralistic modes of resistance that resonate across communities. These women's actions reveal how ethical and relational forms of agency operate both within and beyond carceral and repressive environments, generating new spaces for cross-community alliances and transnational engagement.

Ultimately, this chapter shows that the agency of Bahá'í women, as one illustrative case within a wider landscape of marginalized groups, offers valuable insight into how minority communities negotiate political upheaval and contribute to the formation of emancipatory imaginaries in contemporary Iran and beyond. Their experiences illuminate broader theoretical and methodological questions in minority studies concerning how oppressed groups cultivate resilient subjectivities, build solidarities, and actively participate in shaping more inclusive and just futures.

Reference List

AI-assisted tools, including Grammarly, were used for language editing and structural clarity. The author retained full responsibility for the intellectual content of the chapter.

Abdorrahman Boroumand Center for Human Rights in Iran, and Monash University | Eleos Justice. 2024, October. *Outsiders: Multifaceted Violence against Bahá'ís in the Islamic Republic of Iran.* https://www.iranrights.org/attachments/library/doc_1165.pdf.

Ahmed, Sara. 2012. *On Being Included: Racism and Diversity in Institutional Life*. Durham, NC: Duke University Press.

Bahá'í International Community. 2005. *Bahá'í Elections and Partisanship: A Compilation.* Haifa: Bahá'í World Centre.

Bahá'í International Community. 2022. *An Unbelievable Injustice: Mahvash Sabet and Fariba Kamalabadi Sentenced to a Second Decade in Prison in Iran.* December 11, 2022. Geneva: Bahá'í International Community. https://www.bic.org/news/unbelievable-injustice-mahvash-sabet-and-fariba-kamalabadi-sentenced-second-decade-prison-iran.

Bahá'í International Community (BIC). 2023. *#OurStoryIsOne Campaign Press Release*. https://news.Bahá'í.org.

Cordesman, Anthony H. 2003. *Saudi Arabia Enters the Twenty-First Century: The Military and International Security Dimensions*. Vol. 1. Westport, CT: Praeger Publishers.

Della Porta, Donatella, and Mario Diani. 2006. *Social Movements: An Introduction.* 2nd ed. Malden, MA: Wiley-Blackwell.

Fahandej, Simin. 2023. "Public Statement at the United Nations Human Rights Council, Geneva." September 15, 2023. Bahá'í International Community – Human Rights.

Foucault, Michel. 1991. *The Foucault Effect: Studies in Governmentality.* Edited by Graham Burchell, Colin Gordon, and Peter Miller. Chicago: University of Chicago Press.

Fraser, Nancy. 1995. "Politics, Culture, and the Public Sphere: Toward a Postmodern Conception." In *Justice Interruptus: Critical Reflections on the "Postsocialist" Condition*, 69–98. New York: Routledge.

Galtung, Johan. 1969. "Violence, Peace, and Peace Research." *Journal of Peace Research* 6 (3): 167–191. https://doi.org/10.1177/002234336900600301.

Harders, Cilja, Annette Jünemann, and Lina Khatib. 2017. "Europe and the Arab World: Neighbours and Uneasy Partners in a Highly Conflictual Context." *International Politics* 54: 434–452. https://doi.org/10.1057/s41311-017-0047-7.

Karlberg, Michael. 2010. Constructive Resilience: The Bahá'í Response to Oppression. *Peace & Change* 35 (2): 222–257.

Keck, Margaret E., and Kathryn Sikkink. 1998. *Activists beyond Borders: Advocacy Networks in International Politics*. Ithaca, NY: Cornell University Press.

Mohanty, Chandra Talpade. 2003. *Feminism Without Borders: Decolonizing Theory, Practicing Solidarity*. Durham, NC: Duke University Press.

Packer, H. 2022. "Iran Students Abroad Stand in Solidarity as Peers Lead Uprisings." *The PIE News*. https://thepienews.com/news/iran-students-solidarity-uprisings/.

Smith, Peter. 2008. *An Introduction to the Bahá'í Faith*. Cambridge: Cambridge University Press.

Tarrow, Sidney. 1998. *Power in Movement: Social Movements and Contentious Politics*. 2nd ed. Cambridge: Cambridge University Press.

3 Enduring Persecution

The Iranian Bahá'í Community's Struggle Since the Mid-1800s

Introduction

The Bahá'í Faith, a globally recognized independent religion, traces its origins to nineteenth-century Iran. It emerged with the proclamation of the Báb (born *Seyyed 'Ali Moḥammad Shirazi*; 20 October 1819, Shiraz–9 July 1850, Tabriz), who foretold the coming of Bahá'u'lláh (born *Mirzâ Ḥosein-'Ali Nuri*; 12 November 1817, Tehran, Persia–29 May 1892, Acre, Ottoman Empire), a Persian nobleman who renounced a life of privilege to promote a divine message centered on unity, peace, and justice. Bahá'u'lláh, regarded by Bahá'ís as the most recent in a line of divine messengers, including Abraham, Moses, Zoroaster, Buddha, Christ, and Muhammad, proclaimed the oneness of God, the unity of religions, and the essential interconnectedness of all humanity. At the heart of Bahá'u'lláh's teachings lie foundational principles that underpin the pursuit of a just and unified global society, including the elimination of prejudice, gender equality, the harmony of science and religion, universal education, and the reduction of wealth disparities.[1] He envisioned a world grounded in collective security, ecological sustainability, and a system of global governance founded in justice and the principle of unity.

Today, the Bahá'í Faith is the second most geographically widespread religion, with over eight million adherents in more than 100,000 localities worldwide (Smith 2008). Its followers represent a diverse cross-section of humanity and are actively engaged in grassroots efforts to promote social cohesion, moral education, and sustainable development. Through community-building activities and participation in public discourse, Bahá'ís contribute to addressing global challenges while fostering inclusive, spiritually grounded societies (Bahá'í International Community (BIC) 2020).

1 The oneness of mankind. Universal peace upheld by a world government. Independent investigation of truth. The common foundation of all religions. The essential harmony of science and religion. Equality of men and women. Elimination of prejudice of all kinds. Universal compulsory education. A spiritual solution to the economic problem. A universal auxiliary language. https://bahai.com/principles.html

DOI: 10.4324/9781003567370-4

The Persecution of Bahá'ís and the Early Struggles

The persecution of the Bahá'í community in Iran constitutes one of the most enduring and systematic campaigns of religious repression in modern history. This persecution began in the mid-nineteenth century with the execution of the Báb and intensified following Bahá'u'lláh's public proclamation of a new divine message. In 1868, Bahá'u'lláh and his family were exiled and imprisoned in the penal city of Acre, within the Ottoman Empire. Despite his confinement until his death in 1892, the Bahá'í Faith continued to expand beyond the borders of Persia, reaching communities throughout the Middle East and eventually across Europe and the wider world (Smith 2008). However, the Bahá'í Faith was met with hostility by the Persian monarchy and the Shia clerical establishment, both of which viewed the new religion as a theological and sociopolitical threat. The violent outbreaks against Bahá'ís, such as the 1903 pogrom in Yazd that claimed the lives of over one hundred individuals,[2] exemplify the intersection of religious intolerance and state complicity (Smith 2008). These acts of violence were not isolated events but part of a broader, systematic strategy of marginalization and suppression, implemented through both overt brutality and entrenched institutional discrimination.

In the early twentieth century, despite ongoing persecution, the Iranian Bahá'í community made notable progress in the sphere of education. Bahá'í schools, recognized for their emphasis on gender equality and inclusive curricula, attracted a substantial number of students from diverse backgrounds, reportedly enrolling a significant portion of the schoolchildren at their peak (Cole 1998; Shahvar 2009). Nevertheless, these achievements were systematically dismantled by the state. In 1934, under the orders of Reza Shah, all Bahá'í schools were forcibly closed, marking a significant escalation in the state's campaign to undermine Bahá'í societal participation (Shahvar 2009).

Subsequent acts of violence and marginalization in the 1940s and 1950s were enabled by a broader climate of state-sanctioned intolerance. In 1944, a mob destroyed a Bahá'í center in Abadih, incited by clerical rhetoric that painted Bahá'ís as heretical enemies of Islam (BIC 2016). By 1955, anti-Bahá'í propaganda was being broadcast on national radio, with government authorization, leading to widespread attacks on individuals and properties.[3]

2 Eyewitness accounts and historical analyses detail how mobs, often encouraged by religious leaders, targeted Bahá'í homes and individuals, leading to widespread killings and destruction of property. The lack of intervention by governmental forces during these attacks suggests a tacit approval or at least a willful negligence on the part of the state, highlighting the systemic nature of the persecution. https://iranpresswatch.org/post/4536/abdul-baha-on-bahai-persecutions-in-1903-part-1/?utm_source=chatgpt.com

3 During Ramadan of that year, Sheikh Mohammad Taqi Falsafi, a prominent preacher, delivered inflammatory sermons against Bahá'ís, which were aired nationwide. These broadcasts incited violence, resulting in numerous Bahá'ís being beaten, their homes and shops looted and burned, and Bahá'í women subjected to abduction and forced marriages with Muslims.

During the 1950s, the fundamentalist Islamic organization *Hojjatiyeh*[4] was established, with its primary objective being the opposition to the Bahá'í Faith. Members of this group infiltrated Bahá'í communities, and many subsequent arrests, imprisonments, and executions of Bahá'ís have been linked to the group's access to Bahá'í membership records. Moreover, during the Pahlavi era, *Hojjatiyeh* appears to have collaborated with *SAVAK*, the Shah's intelligence agency, which had collected data on the religious affiliations of Iranian citizens. This cooperation likely facilitated targeted actions against the Bahá'í community, further intensifying their persecution (Sanasarian 2000).

The Pahlavi era exemplifies how state and religious institutions can converge, even amid ideological tensions, to construct a homogenized national identity that systematically marginalizes religious minorities. As Faghfoory (1987) notes, Reza Shah initially collaborated with the Shiʿa ulama to consolidate political authority between 1921 and 1941. Yet as secular reforms expanded, targeting religious education, dress codes, and the judiciary, the influence of traditional clerical elites was strategically curtailed. This transition reflects the pattern of authoritarian modernization (Gerschenkron 1962; Huntington 1968), wherein states adopt modernizing reforms to enhance control while suppressing ideologies or institutions that might compete with centralized authority.

Within this framework, the Bahá'í Faith functioned not merely as a religious minority but as a philosophical alternative to both the clerical and statist constructions of Iranian identity. While certain Bahá'í principles, such as gender equality, universal literacy, and grassroots community development, converged with elements of the state's modernization agenda, the Faith's spiritual universalism and decentralized model of religious authority fundamentally diverged from the nationalist and theocratic binaries that shaped Pahlavi ideology. As a result, the Bahá'í community occupied a doubly marginalized position: religiously excluded by the clerical establishment (ulama) and politically sidelined by the state.

From the perspective of ideological boundary maintenance (Barth 1969), the repression of Bahá'ís in Iran can be interpreted as a deliberate strategy to delineate the contours of national belonging.[5] The state's violent and

---

The situation escalated to the extent that the National Bahá'í Center in Tehran was occupied by military forces, and its dome was demolished under the supervision of high-ranking officials (Sanasarian 2000, 116–123).

4 The Hojjatiyeh Society, founded in 1953, was a clandestine fundamentalist organization dedicated to combating the Bahá'í Faith. Though officially dissolved in the 1980s, its anti-Bahá'í ideology has had a lasting influence on segments of Iran's clerical and security institutions (Sanasarian 2000).

5 Fredrik Barth's (1969) theory of boundary maintenance argues that ethnic or ideological groups sustain distinct identities by managing symbolic and social boundaries rather than relying solely on cultural content. Applying this to Iran, scholars such as Sanasarian (2000) show how the

institutional responses, ranging from the 1903 Yazd pogrom to the 1934 closure of Bahá'í schools, functioned as boundary-making practices that sought to exclude spiritual and civic alternatives deemed incompatible with the hegemonic vision of "Iranian identity." This repression was not merely reactive but preemptive: designed to fortify a model of national modernity grounded in Twelver Shi 'ism and a monolithic conception of citizenship. By eliminating pluralistic expressions of faith and community life, the state aimed to preserve the symbolic coherence and political exclusivity of its ideological project.

Post-1979 Persecution: From Mob Violence to State Policy

Although the 1979 Islamic Revolution signaled a profound ideological rupture, from secular authoritarianism to theocratic rule, it ultimately preserved and intensified the structural logic of Bahá'í exclusion, embedding it more deeply within the apparatus of state power. The transition from monarchy to theocracy deepened and institutionalized the mechanisms of marginalization, embedding them within a religious-legal framework that endowed discrimination with both spiritual and constitutional legitimacy. This continuity affirms what scholars of authoritarian resilience argue: that political regimes often reconfigure rather than dismantle repressive infrastructures to preserve ideological control (Levitsky and Way 2002).

Drawing on Mahmood Mamdani's (2012) concept of *define and rule*, the Islamic Republic has framed the Bahá'ís not as a legitimate religious minority, but as members of a "deviant sect," blurring the boundary between theological heresy and political treason. This narrative legitimizes their persecution as both a religious obligation and a matter of national security. In 1978 alone, at least seven Bahá'ís were killed in mob violence instigated by clerical authorities (BIC 1993). In fact, after the 1979 Revolution, repression became institutionalized: anti-Bahá'í sentiment was embedded in the Islamic Republic's legal and political framework. Unlike earlier regimes that occasionally exploited anti-Bahá'í rhetoric, the new clerical establishment held a deep ideological hostility toward the Bahá'í Faith. The 1979 Constitution, while recognizing Christians, Jews, and Zoroastrians, made no provision for the Bahá'ís, rendering Iran's largest non-Muslim religious minority legally invisible. This omission has enabled courts to deny Bahá'ís legal protection, including the right to seek justice for violence, murder, or property destruction.[6]

Following this legal marginalization, the Bahá'í community experienced a swift and severe deterioration in its societal position. One of the first symbolic

Islamic Republic utilizes religious exclusion to demarcate "acceptable" national identity and suppress dissenting civic models.

6 https://publications.parliament.uk/pa/cm200203/cmselect/cmfaff/405/405we06.htm?utm_source=chatgpt.com

acts of religious repression was the destruction of the House of the Báb in Shiraz, one of the holiest sites in the Bahá'í Faith, in September 1979 (BIC 2016). Subsequently, a directive from the Ministry of Education in November 1979 mandated the dismissal of all Bahá'í educators and required them to repay previously earned salaries (BIC 2016). That same year, at least seven Bahá'ís were killed, including two who were executed by the state. From 1980 onward, the government escalated its campaign by systematically targeting the elected and appointed leadership of the Bahá'í community. On 21 August 1980, all nine members of the National Spiritual Assembly[7] of the Bahá'ís of Iran were abducted and never seen again, an act widely believed to be an extrajudicial execution. By the end of that year, at least 24 Bahá'ís had been killed, 20 of them by state execution (Iran Human Rights Documentation Center 2007; BIC 2016).

This pattern of execution and intimidation persisted in the years following. In 1981 alone, 48 Bahá'ís were killed, including 8 members of a reconstituted National Spiritual Assembly. The following years saw continued violence: 32 Bahá'ís were killed in 1982, 29 in 1983, and 30 in 1984. Notably, in 1984, despite the formal dissolution of Bahá'í administrative institutions at the government's request, four members of the "third" National Spiritual Assembly were executed (Iran Human Rights Documentation Center 2007; BIC 2016). The sustained persecution of the Bahá'í community in Iran cannot be attributed merely to political or administrative activities; rather, it is rooted in the intrinsic aspects of their religious identity. This aligns with theoretical frameworks on identity-based discrimination, particularly Schermerhorn's (1970) theory of social identity, which posits that marginalized groups are often targeted when their cultural or religious values diverge from those of the dominant group. In this context, the Bahá'ís' distinct theological principles, such as the recognition of a post-Islamic prophetic figure and rejection of clerical hierarchy, posed a symbolic challenge to the Islamic Republic's ideological framework. This theoretical lens emphasizes how identity itself becomes a site of contestation and repression, reinforcing the idea that the persecution of the Bahá'ís is best understood as a form of religiously motivated social exclusion rather than conventional political dissent.

Perhaps the most harrowing episode occurred in June 1983, when ten Bahá'í women, most in their twenties and one as young as 17, were executed by hanging.[8] Their primary "offense" was conducting Bahá'í children's

7 At the national level, the affairs of the Bahá'í community are administered by the National Spiritual Assembly, a nine-member elected council responsible for guiding, coordinating, and stimulating the activities of Local Spiritual Assemblies and individual members of the Bahá'í community within a given country.

8 Their narratives are part of next chapter. https://iranhrdc.org/wp-content/uploads/PUBLIC/pdf/1323438331307-tiffdocs.pdf

classes and engaging in activities in the Bahá'í community. Prior to their execution, they were subjected to physical and psychological torture in an attempt to force them into renouncing their faith. Like many other Bahá'ís arrested over the decades, they refused. The state's consistent offering of mercy in exchange for recantation serves as compelling evidence that the persecution has been driven exclusively by religious intolerance.

The severity of these abuses eventually garnered widespread international condemnation. Coverage in global media, resolutions from the United Nations, and advocacy from human rights organizations compelled the Iranian government to reduce the frequency of executions and mass imprisonments. However, this shift in tactics did not signify a reversal of policy. Instead, the state adopted a more subtle and insidious form of repression, focusing on socioeconomic exclusion. This revised strategy was codified in the 1991 government memorandum known as *The Bahá'í Question*,[9] which continues to inform Iran's discriminatory policies against Bahá'ís (BIC 1993).

Escalations, Complexities, and Shifting State Policies

Following the cessation of large-scale executions, a marked shift in state policy toward the Bahá'í community in Iran has become evident. This shift signaled not a retreat from persecution but a transformation in its modalities, prioritizing the physical marginalization and epistemic erasure of Bahá'ís from public life embedded within state structures. This evolving approach includes the implementation of discriminatory legal frameworks, the circulation of government directives, economic strangulation, denial of access to higher education, employment restrictions, arbitrary arrests, covert identification and surveillance, and the suppression of religious and cultural expression (BIC 1993; Iran Human Rights Documentation Center 2007). In what follows, these mechanisms are examined through selected case studies and relevant documentary evidence.

Discriminatory Legal Instruments

The legal framework in Iran systematically marginalizes and discriminates against the Bahá'í community, with the country's constitution playing a central role in institutionalizing this exclusion. Article 4 of the Iranian Constitution mandates that all laws must conform to Islamic criteria, reinforcing the exclusion of Bahá'ís. Additionally, Article 13 acknowledges certain religious minorities but fails to extend this recognition to the Bahá'í community, despite it being the largest non-Muslim minority in the country. As noted by Shahin Milani (2016), a legal analyst at the Iran Human Rights

9 https://news.bahai.org/human-rights/iran/the-bahai-question

Documentation Center, this omission fosters "institutionalized religious discrimination" against Bahá'ís. Milani further argues that this legal framework aligns with Iran's broader goal of maintaining a national identity as an Islamic Republic, wherein the marginalization of Bahá'ís is systematically reinforced by both state laws and religious edicts from senior clerics.[10]

Moreover, Article 19 of the Iranian Constitution guarantees equal rights to all Iranians regardless of ethnicity or tribe. However, the lack of a reference to religion opens the door to discrimination based on religious beliefs, as evidenced by the consistent denial of civil rights for Bahá'ís. Despite official denials of discrimination, numerous government documents, including the 1991 memorandum titled *The Bahá'í Question*, issued in 1991, codified a national policy of discrimination against the Bahá'í community. This document remains in force, with subsequent state directives reinforcing its core strategies. Notable examples include a 2005 letter from Iranian military headquarters instructing intelligence agencies to monitor Bahá'í activity (BIC 2006a), a 2006 directive from the Ministry of Science mandating the expulsion of Bahá'í students from universities (United Nations General Assembly 2007), and a 2007 letter imposing professional restrictions on Bahá'ís (UN Human Rights Council 2008). Regional documents further demonstrate the policy's local enforcement, including a 2009 letter from Kerman Province restricting Bahá'ís from acquiring property (BIC 2010b), and a 2020 directive from Sari officials calling for surveillance and forced conversion of Bahá'í students (BIC 2021). The codification of anti-Bahá'í policies through national and local directives reflects how authoritarian states use bureaucratic repression to legitimize exclusion. Drawing on Weber's theory of rational-legal authority, the Islamic Republic disguises religious discrimination as routine governance (Weber 1978).

Fatwas as Instruments of State Power

In Iran, Fatwas issued by senior clerics can carry legal weight and significantly influence or align with state policies, especially when issued by high-ranking figures such as the Supreme Leader. Although fatwas are not codified laws, they serve as religious guidance that shapes public and legal behavior within the Islamic framework. In the case of the Bahá'í community, fatwas have played a key role in systemic discrimination. Fatwas from the highest religious authorities in Iran, including Ayatollah Ali Khamenei, have delegitimized and marginalized Bahá'ís, labeling them as "deviant," "misguided," or "unclean." This religious vilification has not only contributed to the dehumanization of Bahá'ís but has also reinforced their exclusion from Iranian society,

10 https://iranhrdc.org/blocked-from-progress-persecution-of-irans-bahai-community-since-1979/?utm_source=chatgpt.com

further entrenching their persecution. Ayatollah Khamenei has declared that "all members of the perverse Bahá'íst sect are condemned as blasphemous and ritually unclean," emphasizing that any items contaminated by contact with Bahá'ís should be avoided. Such language not only denies the humanity of Bahá'ís but actively encourages social and religious ostracism (BIC 2006a). Similarly, Ayatollah Behjat's fatwa asserts that "Bahá'ís are unclean and association with them must be avoided," reinforcing the view that any interaction with Bahá'ís is both morally and religiously inappropriate (BIC 2006b).

Ayatollah Makarem Shirazi's 2007 fatwa prohibits association with Bahá'ís, except when it is deemed a religious duty to "guide them to the right path," thereby positioning the Bahá'í community as both religiously inferior and in need of conversion. The fatwa issued by Ayatollah Nouri Hamadani in 2010 furthers this dehumanization, describing Bahá'ís as "more unclean than dogs," a comparison that signifies the extreme level of disdain directed toward them. Khamenei reiterated this sentiment in a fatwa issued in 2018, instructing that "association and dealings with this perverse and misguided sect" should be strictly avoided (BIC 2006b). In sum, the use of fatwas to marginalize the Bahá'í community in Iran exemplifies the fusion of religious doctrine and state power within a broader project of religious nationalism. These clerical rulings, far from being isolated theological opinions, function as strategic instruments of symbolic and cultural violence (Bourdieu 1991; Galtung 1969), reinforcing the Islamic Republic's ideological boundaries. By constructing the Bahá'ís as religiously impure and socially illegitimate, the regime sustains a model of national identity that depends on exclusion and othering. This convergence of clerical authority and political repression illustrates how theocratic regimes weaponize religious discourse to entrench power, suppress pluralism, and manufacture a homogenized national community.

Detention and Incarceration: Mechanisms of Control

Although international pressure curtailed executions in the 1980s, persecution has continued in other forms, especially arbitrary detention. Despite the Bahá'ís' well-documented commitment to nonviolence and political neutrality in civic service, members are regularly arrested without due process, subjected to psychological and physical abuse, and imprisoned on fabricated charges. These arrests frequently coincide with periods of political unrest, wherein Bahá'ís are scapegoated as subversive threats, an accusation that starkly contradicts the community's principles of lawful obedience and constructive social engagement (Iran Human Rights Documentation Center 2007; BIC 2023).[11]

11 seethisalsohttps://www.hrw.org/news/2024/04/01/iran-persecution-bahais?utm_source=chatgpt.com, https://www.bic.org/media/scapegoating-irans-bahais?utm_source=chatgpt.com

A clear example of systematic harassment is evident at every stage of arrest and imprisonment of Bahá'ís in Iran. Judicial and penal practices routinely involve prolonged pre-trial detention, excessive bail demands, denial of legal representation, coerced confessions, and solitary confinement – all in violation of basic legal safeguards. In 2022, this repression escalated to include the arrest of minors and mass detentions, demonstrating the state's willingness to apply punitive measures indiscriminately, irrespective of age or evidence (BIC 2022a). These actions violate Article 18 of the *International Covenant on Civil and Political Rights* (ICCPR), to which Iran is a state party, guaranteeing freedom of religion and belief (UN General Assembly 1966).

Legal proceedings against Bahá'ís also reveal deep-seated institutional bias. Charges are frequently grounded in religious identity alone, with courts often framing belief in Bahá'í teachings as "propaganda against the regime." Sentences are imposed not for criminal activity but for peaceful engagement in community service, education, and spiritual development. A stark example occurred in Gorgan, where 24 Bahá'ís were collectively sentenced to 193 years in prison for participating in religious gatherings and children's classes (BIC 2022a). Even legal defenders of Bahá'í clients are targeted. Lawyers face harassment, threats, restricted access to legal files, and pressure to withdraw from cases. Judicial authorities routinely express overt religious bias, including refusals to read Bahá'í materials and the use of discriminatory or mocking language in courtrooms (Iran Human Rights Documentation Center 2007).

The systemic persecution of Bahá'ís in Iran mirrors patterns observed in other contexts where religious identity is constructed as a threat to state ideology. Similar tactics have been employed against Rohingya Muslims in Myanmar, Uighur Muslims in China, and Ahmadiyya Muslims in Pakistan, where legal systems, surveillance apparatuses, and nationalist rhetoric have been weaponized to marginalize religious minorities. What distinguishes the Iranian case, however, is the combination of theocratic doctrine with bureaucratic power, where fatwas, legal rulings, and policy documents work in concert to justify and perpetuate exclusion.

Identification and Monitoring

Over the past two decades, Iranian authorities have systematically issued directives instructing law enforcement, intelligence agencies, and other state

For example, during periods of political instability, such as the 2009 Green Movement, numerous Bahá'í individuals were arrested under accusations of being involved in anti-government activities, despite their apolitical stance and commitment to non-interference in politics. Similarly, in 2011, 2017–2018, 2019–2020, and 2021–2022 a wave of arrests targeted Bahá'í community members, including educators and business owners under the guise of national security threats, even though their actions were solely focused on promoting education and welfare within their community. https://www.iranrights.org/library/document/4533, https://www.rferl.org/a/Iranian_Police_Arrest_Bahais_Ahead_Of_Protests/1955669.html?utm_source=chatgpt.com institutions to identify, monitor, and restrict individuals solely based on their adherence to the Bahá'í Faith. These actions represent a flagrant violation of the right to privacy and exemplify state-sanctioned religious discrimination. A particularly illustrative case is a confidential directive dated 29 October 2005 from Iran's military headquarters, which called upon intelligence and security bodies, including the police and the Islamic Revolutionary Guard Corps, to identify members of the Bahá'í community and monitor their activities (BIC 2006c).

The existence of this directive was publicly disclosed in March 2006 by Asma Jahangir,[12] then the United Nations Special Rapporteur on freedom of religion or belief, who described the surveillance order as "an impermissible and unacceptable interference" with the rights of religious minorities and warned that it could intensify persecution (BIC 2006d). Further evidence of this state-directed surveillance appears in a 9 April 2007 directive to police commanders, ordering the "ongoing monitoring and supervision" of Bahá'í activities (BIC 2007).

In a notable case from 2021, the League for the Defence of Human Rights in Iran (LDDHI) and the International Federation for Human Rights (FIDH) exposed an official directive originating from the city of Sari, Mazandaran Province. Dated 21 September 2020, the document called for "strict controls" on the Bahá'í population, including the identification of Bahá'í students with the intent of converting them to Islam, and surveillance of their public and private gatherings. Crucially, this directive was issued by the Commission on Ethnicities, Sects, and Religions, operating under the Supreme National Security Council, an institution chaired by the president of Iran and tasked with national security management. The involvement of this high-level body underscores the strategic and coordinated nature of the state's campaign against the Bahá'ís (FIDH and LDDHI 2021).

Recent reports confirm the continuation of such discriminatory practices. In 2022, Bahá'ís residing in Sanandaj and other Kurdish-majority regions faced constant surveillance and intimidation (Hana Human Rights Organization 2022). In August 2023, authorities in Sistan and Baluchistan installed security cameras aimed at Bahá'í residences to monitor their movements. In some cases, detainees were subjected to degrading surveillance measures, including electronic ankle monitors intended to track and restrict their freedom of movement (Shabtab News 2023).

12 She was a Pakistani jurist, lawyer, and human rights activist who dedicated her career to defending marginalized and underprivileged communities. Through the provision of free legal aid and the establishment of shelters, she supported vulnerable populations while actively challenging the oppression of religious minorities, honor-based violence, and the treatment of prisoners within Pakistan's penal system.

These practices represent a direct violation of religious freedom under Article 18 of the International Covenant on Civil and Political Rights (UN General Assembly 1966). By framing Bahá'í identity as a security threat, the Iranian state transforms faith into a punishable offense. The coordination between high-level security institutions and local authorities reveals a systematic intent not merely to monitor the Bahá'í community, but to suppress its social presence and spiritual identity. In this context, the Iranian government's treatment of Bahá'ís exemplifies how religious repression is embedded within modern authoritarian statecraft, not through overt theocratic decrees alone, but via legalistic, securitized, and technologized practices that erode fundamental human rights under the guise of governance.

Institutionalized Educational Discrimination

The systematic exclusion of Bahá'ís from higher education in Iran exemplifies state-sanctioned structural discrimination, breaking Iran's obligations under the *Universal Declaration of Human Rights* and the *International Covenant on Civil and Political Rights*, which guarantee the rights to education and freedom of religion. Since the 1979 Islamic Revolution, Bahá'ís in Iran have faced entrenched institutional barriers to higher education, marking one of the most systematic forms of state-sponsored discrimination against the community. A 1991 confidential memorandum, approved by Supreme Leader Ayatollah Khamenei, explicitly instructed authorities to block the progress and development of Bahá'ís, including denying them access to universities. Even after the formal removal in 2004 of the requirements to declare religious affiliation to participate in the university entrance exam, exclusion persisted through covert bureaucratic obstruction. Student applications were routinely labeled as "incomplete" or rejected on vague grounds. A 2006 directive from the Ministry of Science, Research, and Technology mandated the expulsion of any student identified as a Bahá'í, regardless of their academic performance. In 2023, a new form of exclusion emerged, in which Bahá'í applicants were compelled to renounce key elements of their faith as a precondition for university enrollment.

Beyond institutional exclusion, the content of Iran's national curriculum plays a critical role in the symbolic marginalization of Bahá'í identity. Textbooks at the junior high and high school levels frequently depict the Bahá'í Faith as a foreign construct, falsely attributing its origins to colonial powers purportedly seeking to undermine Islam. These narratives function as mechanisms of ideological control, disseminating misinformation that delegitimizes the Bahá'í Faith while fostering suspicion and animosity toward its adherents within educational materials targeting children and youth.[13] In response to

13 see https://www.refworld.org/reference/countryrep/freehou/2008/en/58927?utm_source=chatgpt.com

their systemic exclusion from Iran's higher education system, the Bahá'í community established the Bahá'í Institute for Higher Education (BIHE) in 1987 as a form of nonviolent resistance and educational self-determination.[14] Functioning through decentralized networks and volunteer faculty, BIHE offers alternative academic pathways for Bahá'í youth, embodying what scholars' term *constructive resilience*, a proactive strategy to counter repression through capacity-building and community empowerment (Karlberg 2010).

Initially reliant on correspondence courses, BIHE gradually expanded to include in-person classes and, later, advanced digital platforms. A key development has been the formation of an Affiliated Global Faculty (AGF), consisting of hundreds of academics from international universities who contribute as instructors, mentors, and advisors. Despite lacking formal recognition by the Iranian state, BIHE has earned global credibility: over 100 accredited institutions in Europe and North America have accepted its graduates for postgraduate study.[15] Admissions decisions are often made on a case-by-case basis, reflecting the recognized academic rigor and success of BIHE alumni in both academia and professional sectors. Thus, BIHE serves not only as an educational initiative but also as a symbol of resistance to ideological repression. It exemplifies how marginalized communities can mobilize intellectual and social capital to foster educational access, social resilience, and global solidarity under conditions of systemic exclusion.

Persistent and Intensified State Propaganda

The systematic persecution of the Bahá'í community in Iran has been strengthened by a long-standing, state-sponsored campaign of propaganda and hate speech. This strategy is explicitly outlined in the confidential 1991 confidential memorandum, which instructed officials to block Bahá'ís from social and economic advancement and to "counter their propaganda" (BIC 1993). Since the 1979 Islamic Revolution, Iranian state-controlled media, including television, print, and digital platforms, have served as tools to delegitimize the Bahá'í Faith. These propaganda efforts often coincide with escalated waves of persecution, reflecting what sociologists might describe as a cyclical mobilization of symbolic violence (Bourdieu 1991; Galtung 1969). A striking example occurred in July 2022, when Iranian authorities launched a coordinated media and security operation targeting Bahá'í educators. Raids on preschools were paired with staged disinformation claiming religious conversion of Muslim children, falsely presented through manipulated audiovisual "evidence" (BIC 2022b, 2022c). Such

14 https://www.bihe.org/about/vision-and-mission
15 https://www.bihe.org/international-recognition

portrayals rely on recurring tropes: labeling Bahá'ís as heretical, morally corrupt, or aligned with foreign powers, especially Zionism.

The BIC has consistently documented the recurrence of such defamatory narratives, which rely on a range of themes. These include accusations that the Bahá'í Faith is a deviant sect; that its adherents are morally corrupt, anti-Islamic, or politically subversive; and that they maintain ties with foreign powers, including Western states and Zionist entities. These claims are systematically constructed and lack evidentiary support, functioning primarily as ideological tools to justify the Bahá'ís' exclusion from civic life. For instance, the Bahá'í marriage ceremony, which is not recognized by Iranian authorities, has been weaponized in propaganda efforts to portray Bahá'í women as immoral. Similarly, gender-integrated gatherings have been framed as licentious, despite the community's adherence to strict ethical standards.

Claims that Bahá'ís aim to undermine Islam or serve as member of SAVAK[16] and agents of Zionism are historically and theologically unfounded. Theologically, the Bahá'í Faith affirms the prophetic role of Muhammad and regards the Qur'an with reverence alongside other sacred texts (Karlberg 2010; Shahvar 2009). The presence of the administrative buildings of the Bahá'í World Centre in Israel is frequently invoked in anti-Bahá'í propaganda. However, it is the historical consequence of Bahá'u'lláh's exile to Ottoman Palestine by Qajar authorities, in concert with Muslim religious leaders of the time, well before the establishment of the modern Israeli state. This critical context is deliberately omitted in Iranian media narratives to incite nationalist and sectarian antagonism (Masumian 2009).

Further claims that Bahá'ís collaborated with SAVAK or support foreign opposition movements are also unsupported by evidence. In fact, during both the Pahlavi era and under the Islamic Republic, the Bahá'í community has maintained a consistent posture of political noninvolvement, aligned with core teachings that prohibit partisanship and require obedience to the state unless religious principles are violated (Karlberg 2010; Sanasarian 2000). Moreover, accusations of ties to Zionism or foreign intelligence are politically expedient myths, frequently employed to justify repression, yet systematically debunked by both academic research and international human rights bodies (Shahvar 2009).

These claims, lacking any basis in empirical reality, function instead as ideological instruments aimed at delegitimizing the Bahá'í community and rationalizing their systematic exclusion from public life. By framing Bahá'ís as threats to both religious integrity and national security, the state deploys orchestrated disinformation campaigns that conflate political authority with religious orthodoxy. Such propaganda does not incidentally form a central mechanism within a broader architecture of ideological and structural violence. Viewed through the conceptual lenses of symbolic violence and authoritarian power, these accounts

16 SAVAK was the Iranian security police during the reign of Shah Mohammad Reza Pahlavi.

reveal how regimes weaponize discourse to construct internal "others," normalize coercive forms of governance, and institutionalize exclusionary nationalism. In doing so, they reaffirm the argument advanced in the Introduction: that the marginalization of the Bahá'í community is not merely a byproduct of political or religious intolerance, but a deliberate and strategic process through which authoritarian systems reproduce their own legitimacy.

Discursive Demonization and State Power

This propaganda is not merely peripheral; it is endorsed and reproduced at the highest levels of political and religious authority. In a nationally televised speech in October 2010, Ali Khamenei explicitly labeled Bahá'ís as "enemies of the Islamic Revolution," issuing fatwas that prohibit any form of social, economic, or religious interaction with them. Echoed by senior clerics, these rulings codify Bahá'í exclusion across both public and private spheres. The repetition of such narratives across state-controlled media and religious platforms constructs Bahá'ís as ontological outsiders, permanently alien to the moral and political identity of the Islamic Republic. Clerics such as Mohammad Kamalvand and Jadeed Benab further reinforce this demonization by portraying Bahá'ís as agents of Zionism and foreign powers, framing them as existential threats to national sovereignty and religious purity (BIC 2023).

Yet this state-driven narrative often contrasts sharply with lived realities in Iran, where everyday interactions between Bahá'ís and Muslims have historically reflected more nuanced, and at times cooperative, social relationships. Recognizing this disjuncture underscores how authoritarian regimes construct ideological boundaries that do not necessarily align with the complexities of social life. The insistence on portraying Bahá'ís as existential threats thus reveals less about intercommunal relations than about the political utility of such narratives in consolidating power, policing religious identity, and sustaining exclusionary national imaginaries.

One of the most illustrative cases of the tension between state propaganda and individual conscience is the 2016 meeting between Fariba Kamalabadi, a prominent Bahá'í prisoner on temporary furlough, and Faezeh Hashemi, the daughter of former President Rafsanjani and herself a former political prisoner. Their personal act of solidarity provoked a torrent of denunciation from Iranian officials, clerics, and media outlets. Judiciary spokesman Gholamhossein Mohseni Ejei called the meeting "a very ugly and obscene act," while other officials accused Hashemi of treason. This reaction revealed not only the extent of the state's hostility toward the Bahá'í Faith but also the high political cost of any perceived deviation from its anti-Bahá'í orthodoxy.[17]

17 see https://iranhumanrights.org/2016/06/cartoon-146/, https://news.bahai.org/story/1108/reaction-meeting-with-bahai-exposes-truth

The demonization of Bahá'ís as foreign agents or morally impure has direct and dangerous consequences. Hate speech and religious decrees contribute to a climate of impunity in which violence against Bahá'ís is normalized. Numerous incidents illustrate this pattern. Between 2005 and 2014, the Bahá'í community in Iran endured over 50 documented physical assaults, none of which resulted in the prosecution or punishment of the perpetrators. Additionally, at least nine Bahá'ís were murdered under suspicious circumstances during this period, with the assailants similarly enjoying impunity.[18]

The persecution of Bahá'ís in Iran extends beyond institutional discrimination to include widespread community-level harassment. Families report receiving death threats, verbal abuse, and vandalism, such as the 2010 arson attack on Bahá'í-owned businesses in Rafsanjan.[19] In 2014, the Moodi family in Birjand was brutally attacked in their home by a masked assailant.[20] In July 2022, shortly after a surge of anti-Bahá'í rhetoric, the Ministry of Intelligence conducted raids on over 50 Bahá'í homes and businesses across the country, detaining 13 individuals. The Ministry justified these actions by falsely framing the Bahá'í community as a "Zionist espionage network" infiltrating educational spaces, an accusation reminiscent of earlier anti-Semitic and colonialist conspiracies.[21] Misrepresentation of Bahá'í identity in Iran is not merely a manifestation of religious intolerance but a deliberate strategy of social exclusion and ideological control. This pattern of unaddressed violence reflects a broader state policy of passive tolerance or tacit endorsement of anti-Bahá'í aggression. The result has been a pervasive climate of suffering, isolation, and institutional violence, which violates fundamental human rights and religious freedoms for the last four decades.

Economic Marginalization

Historically, members of the Bahá'í community contributed significantly to Iran's social, economic, and intellectual development, establishing modern schools, advancing public-health initiatives, and participating in early

18 https://news.bahai.org/story/979/three-bahais-stabbed-iran-apparently-religious-hate-crime

19 see https://iranbahaipersecution.bic.org/archive/arson-attack-shops-six-bahais-rafsanjan?utm_source=chatgpt.com

20 According to reports from Iran, a masked assailant entered the home of Ghodratollah Moodi and his wife, Touba Sabzehjou, at approximately 8 p.m. The attacker immediately assaulted Mr. Moodi, Mrs. Sabzehjou, and their daughter, Azam Moodi, using a knife or another sharp object, inflicting serious injuries on all three. Mr. Moodi sustained wounds to his abdomen and side, while Mrs. Sabzehjou was severely injured in the neck. Both lost consciousness due to significant blood loss. Despite her own serious injuries, Azam Moodi managed to call the police. All three victims were transported to the hospital, where they remain under close medical supervision. https://news.bahai.org/story/979/three-bahais-stabbed-iran-apparently-religious-hate-crime

21 see https://news.bahai.org/story/1606/fresh-wave-of-arrests-and-raids-across-iran-as-baha-is-absurdly-accused-of-coloni, https://www.jpost.com/middle-east/iran-news/article-716252

reform movements, engagements firmly grounded in Bahá'í teachings that regard productive work, craftsmanship, and professional service as forms of worship and essential acts of social responsibility (Brookshaw and Fazel 2012; Momen 2025; BIC 1984). However, since the establishment of the Islamic Republic in 1979, the Iranian government has systematically denied Bahá'ís this fundamental right. Economic marginalization, including restrictions on employment, entrepreneurship, and professional engagement, has become a key feature of the broader framework of religious persecution they face. Authorities confiscated or froze properties belonging to the Bahá'í community institutions, including savings and investment cooperatives, resulting in the loss of personal savings for an estimated 15,000 individuals. Simultaneously, pension benefits for retired Bahá'ís were terminated, reflecting a broader state policy of marginalization (Zabihi-Moghaddam 2021; Manocha and Tahzib 2018).

By 1980, the regime began purging Bahá'ís from public sector employment, dismissing them from roles in education, healthcare, government ministries, and state-run enterprises. In many cases, individuals were pressured to recant their faith and convert to Islam; refusal was formally used as grounds for dismissal under accusations of holding beliefs "contrary to Islam" (Riazati 2011; Herman 2019).[22] Following these purges, Iranian authorities also targeted the private sector. Bahá'í-owned businesses and factories were either expropriated or shut down, while private companies were pressured to dismiss Bahá'í employees. Banks were instructed to restrict the financial operations of Bahá'ís, and a 1991 government memorandum explicitly mandated denying employment to individuals who identified as Bahá'í. This directive laid the foundation for continued discrimination, including refusal to issue or renew business licenses, closure of Bahá'í-owned businesses, and restrictions on access to key sectors such as hospitality, food services, publishing, and information technology. Landlords were pressured not to renew leases for Bahá'í tenants, and government agencies avoided doing business with Bahá'í entrepreneurs (Ghanea 2015; Zabihi-Moghaddam 2021; Herman 2019). Bureaucratic harassment, such as arbitrary inspections and workplace raids, further enforced these policies. Numerous documented cases demonstrate the consistency of these discriminatory practices.

In 1995, more than 150 Bahá'í properties were reportedly seized in Yazd, including egregious cases such as the eviction of a blind woman from her home, an act that provoked public outcry yet proceeded unimpeded. In 2010, the destruction of approximately 50 Bahá'í homes in Ivel, Mazandaran, reflected both the continuity of dispossession and its communal targeting. Notably, these homes had originally been confiscated in 1983, and despite sustained legal efforts, redress has been consistently

22 This policy of exclusion was codified in 1981 and continues until now.

denied, underscoring the entrenched impunity of anti-Bahá'í measures. In 2012, a hygiene products company in Tehran was shut down, leaving 70 employees unemployed. In 2014, Bahá'í farmers in Semnan were prevented from harvesting their produce based on false accusations of collaboration with Israel. In 2015, a disabled Bahá'í vendor in Sari had his kiosk destroyed multiple times, despite holding official permits. Both he and his wife were pressured to inform on fellow Bahá'ís or renounce their faith in exchange for economic relief but refused (BIC 2010a). In parallel, intelligence forces have persistently raided private residences and workplaces, confiscating religious texts, photographs, electronics, and tools essential to personal livelihood. These intrusions reflect both ideological hostility and material exploitation. The 2019 raid in Isfahan, which resulted in the seizure of musical instruments and religious items, exemplifies the overlapping motives of repression: erasing cultural expression while weakening economic autonomy (BIC 2023).

A new wave of property seizures was documented in 2021, highlighting the increasing coordination and institutionalization of this practice. Bahá'í farmlands in Kata village were listed for public auction without the consent of their owners, priced well below market value, and restricted from Bahá'í or sympathetic Muslim buyers. These auctions were administered by Setad (The Execution of Imam Khomeini's Order), a powerful economic conglomerate operating under the authority of the Supreme Leader (BIC 2023).[23]

The state also engages in coordinated campaigns to punish Bahá'ís for observing religious holidays. While Iranian trade laws permit the closure of businesses on Bahá'í holy days, at least 86 Bahá'í-owned shops were permanently sealed in 2016 alone after observing these holidays. The justification cited by authorities, violations of trading laws, masked the underlying religiously motivated repression (BIC 2023). In addition to large-scale closures, Bahá'ís routinely face microaggressions in economic life. Bureaucratic barriers, such as delays in renewing licenses, the derogatory labeling of religious identity on official forms, and arbitrary denial of permits, inflict both psychological and financial harm. In Yazd, for example, a taxi driver's license application was rejected after officials labeled him as part of the "perverse sect of Bahá'ísm," while another applicant's religious identity was misclassified and the error was denied correction (BIC 2023).

Beyond economic dispossession, the state's campaign has extended to cultural and spiritual annihilation. The destruction of Bahá'í cemeteries, shrines, and sacred sites represents an effort to erase the memory and presence of the Faith from the national imaginary. A paradigmatic instance occurred in 1979 with the demolition of the House of the Báb in Shiraz, followed by

23 BIC Archives. https://www.bic.org/focus-areas/situation-iranian-bahais, UN OHCHR Reports on Iran. https://www.ohchr.org/en/countri es/iran

subsequent desecrations, including the gravesite of Quddus[24] and the historic residence of Bahá'u'lláh's father correction (BIC 2023). These acts exemplify what scholars describe as cultural genocide, whereby the state targets the symbolic heritage of a group to extinguish its collective identity (Kingston 2015; Davidavičiūtė 2021).

More recently, a pronounced escalation in 2021, evident in coordinated raids across Baharestan, Isfahan, and Shiraz, suggests a renewed state initiative aimed at intensifying the marginalization of Bahá'ís. Legal trials, arbitrary arrests, and the targeting of youth have become common features of this repressive apparatus. In one particularly revealing episode, 13 Bahá'í youth, including two children, were detained in Qaemshahr for engaging in an educational discussion on social progress correction (BIC 2023). This event encapsulates the paradox of persecution: those excluded from formal education are criminalized for pursuing knowledge informally. In August 2022, nearly 200 government agents conducted a coordinated raid in Roshankouh, demolishing six Bahá'í homes and confiscating over 20 hectares of land. The operation was marked by violence, arrests, and the destruction of mobile phones, indicative of a deliberate attempt to suppress evidence and obstruct accountability correction (BIC 2023). These actions are part of a broader securitization of Bahá'í identity, where surveillance and forced displacement intersect to enforce exclusion correction.

From the vantage point of critical political economy, power structures and hegemonic ideologies do not simply legitimize existing social inequality; they actively construct and enforce it by regulating the allocation of resources and opportunities (Cafruny and Ryner 2009; Phillips 2017). In the context of the Islamic Republic of Iran, official religion serves not only as the ideological foundation of the state but also as a decisive criterion of citizenship. This criterion governs access to education, employment, and economic participation, systematically excluding those deemed religiously "other." The Bahá'í community exemplifies the consequences of this structure, enduring a dual crisis: the general economic deterioration affecting the broader Iranian, and a targeted regime of state-sanctioned discrimination.

Unlike overt forms of repression such as imprisonment or societal violence acts, economic exclusion functions with more subtlety, yet delivers enduring harm to minority communities. It limits pathways to economic self-sufficiency, disrupts community-based capital formation, and systematically erases marginalized groups from public and commercial life. These outcomes obstruct the formation of an economically secure middle class and undermine the material preconditions for autonomous political or social agency. In the

24 He is the title of Mullá Muḥammad 'Alí-i-Bárfurúshi, who was the most prominent disciple of the Báb. He was the eighteenth and final Letter of the Living. https://bahai-library.com/hosseini_iranica_quddus

end, the case of the Bahá'ís in Iran offers a stark illustration of how religious identity is weaponized as an instrument of economic control. It reveals the intimate entanglement of ideology, governance, and livelihood, where access to economic life becomes not just a function of market dynamics, but a tool of coercive statecraft and ideological discipline.

Conclusion

The systemic persecution of the Bahá'í community in post-revolutionary Iran reveals how the Islamic Republic deploys confiscation of material assets, civic standing, and ultimately, identity itself, as a deliberate instrument of ideological governance. These practices are not incidental episodes of discrimination but part of a long-standing historical continuum of religious intolerance, institutionalized through legal codes, administrative procedures, and extralegal coercion. In this framework, dispossession functions dually: it undermines the material foundations of Bahá'í life while simultaneously reinforcing the state's claim to religious orthodoxy and national authenticity.

By tracing shifts in state policy across the past four decades, this chapter has shown how the Iranian government regulates populations by constraining religious expression and dismantling alternative sources of moral and spiritual authority. The Bahá'í community, rooted in an independent theological worldview and ethical tradition, is framed as a fundamental challenge to the Islamic Republic's monopoly over moral discourse. Confiscation of homes, businesses, and livelihoods thus becomes not only an economic assault but a targeted attempt to erase Bahá'í presence from the national social imaginary, producing conformity through patterned exclusion and deprivation.

Foucault's notion of governmentality offers a useful lens for interpreting these dynamics: the persecution of the Bahá'ís is not merely sectarian hostility but a rationalized political project aimed at cultivating an ideologically homogeneous citizenry. Under this mode of governance, religious difference is pathologized, dissent is rendered invisible, and minority communities are disciplined through administrative and biopolitical means. Confiscation emerges here as a technique of power that extends beyond the seizure of property to reshape the conditions through which identities are lived and futures envisioned.

Finally, situating these practices within the broader context of political crises, including the intensified repression following the WLF movement, highlights how minority persecution becomes intertwined with state efforts at consolidation and securitization. The fluctuating intensity of anti-Bahá'í campaigns underscores how authoritarian regimes instrumentalize vulnerable communities to reinforce ideological boundaries during moments of national upheaval. In this sense, the modern history of the Iranian Bahá'ís illuminates the broader mechanisms through which theocratic states police identity, manage dissent, and reproduce power through both material and symbolic forms of dispossession.

Reference List

AI-assisted tools, including Grammarly, were used for language editing and structural clarity. The author retained full responsibility for the intellectual content of the chapter.

Bahá'í International Community. 1984. *Social and Economic Development: The Bahá'í Contribution.* https://www.bic.org/statements/social-and-economic-development-bahai-contribution.

Bahá'í International Community. 1993. *Iran's Secret Blueprint for the Destruction of a Religious Community: An Examination of the 1991 "Bahá'í Question" Memorandum.* New York: Bahá'í International Community. https://www.bic.org/sites/default/files/pdf/secret_blueprint_iran_1993.pdf.

Bahá'í International Community. 2006a. *Ayatollah Khamenei's Decree on How to Treat Bahá'ís.* https://iranbahaipersecution.bic.org/archive/ayatollah-khameneis-decree-how-treat-bahais.

Bahá'í International Community. 2006b. *Fatwas of Religious Leaders about Bahá'ism.* https://iranbahaipersecution.bic.org/archive/fatwas-religious-leaders-about-bahaism.

Bahá'í International Community. 2006c. *Letter from Command Headquarters of the Armed Forces Regarding Identification of Bahá'ís.* https://news.bahai.org/story/473.

Bahá'í International Community. 2006d. *UN Expert Voices Concern Over Iran's Anti-Bahá'í Policies.* https://news.bahai.org/story/1237.

Bahá'í International Community. 2007. *Letter to County Police Forces about the "Perverse Bahá'í Sect."* https://www.bic.org/sites/default/files/pdf/iran/9%20April%202007%20letter%20to%20county%20police%20forces%20about%20perverse%20Bahai%20sect%20ENG.pdf.

Bahá'í International Community. 2010a. *Destruction of Bahá'í Homes in Ivel, Mazandaran.* https://news.bahai.org.

Bahá'í International Community. 2010b. *Implementation of Discriminatory Property Laws against Bahá'ís in Kerman Province.* Internal Document Archive.

Bahá'í International Community. 2016. *The Bahá'í Question Revisited: Persecution and Resilience in Iran.* New York: Bahá'í International Community. https://www.bic.org/sites/default/files/pdf/thebahaiquestionrevisited_final_160930e.pdf.

Bahá'í International Community. 2020. *A Governance Befitting: Humanity and the Path Toward a Just Global Order.* New York: Bahá'í International Community. https://www.bic.org/statements/governance-befitting-humanity-and-path-toward-just-global-order.

Bahá'í International Community. 2021. *Surveillance and Forced Conversion Orders in Sari: A New Wave of Pressure on Bahá'í Students.* https://www.bic.org/news/iranian-authorities-call-surveillance-bahai-students.

Bahá'í International Community. 2022a. *24 Bahá'ís in Gorgan Sentenced to 193 Years in Prison.* https://iranbahaipersecution.bic.org/archive/24-bahais-gorgan-sentenced-193-years-prison.

Bahá'í International Community. 2022b. *Baha'is in Iran: Situation Summary.* https://www.bic.org.

Bahá'í International Community. 2022c. *Dozens of Bahá'ís Arbitrarily Detained, Including Minors.* https://www.bic.org/news/dozens-bahais-arbitrarily-detained-iran.

Bahá'í International Community. 2023. *The Bahá'í Question: Cultural Cleansing in Iran*. https://www.bic.org/sites/default/files/pdf/tbq_2023_f_screen.pdf.

Barth, Fredrik. 1969. *Ethnic Groups and Boundaries: The Social Organization of Culture Difference*. Boston: Little, Brown and Company.

Bourdieu, Pierre. 1991. *Language and Symbolic Power*. Edited by John B. Thompson. Translated by Gino Raymond and Matthew Adamson. Cambridge: Harvard University Press.

Brookshaw, Dominic Parviz, and Seena B. Fazel, eds. 2012. *The Bahá'ís of Iran: Socio-Historical Studies*. London: Routledge.

Cafruny, Alan, and Magnus Ryner. 2009. *Critical Political Economy*. https://www.academia.edu/download/37995323/Cafruny_and_Ryner_Critical_Political_Economy.pdf.

Cole, Juan R. I. 1998. *Modernity and the Millennium: The Genesis of the Bahá'í Faith in the Nineteenth-Century Middle East*. New York: Columbia University Press.

Davidavičiūtė, Rūta. 2021. "Cultural Heritage, Genocide, and Normative Agency." *Journal of Applied Philosophy* 38 (3): 399–416. https://doi.org/10.1111/japp.12473.

Faghfoory, Mohammad H. 1987. "The Ulama–State Relations in Iran: 1921–1941." *International Journal of Middle East Studies* 19 (4): 413–432. http://www.jstor.org/stable/163209.

FIDH and LDDHI. 2021. *Iran: High-Level State Committee Involved in Persecution of Bahá'ís*. https://www.fidh.org/en/issues/human-rights-defenders/iran-high-level-state-committee-involved-in-persecution-of-baha-is-new.

Galtung, Johan. 1969. "Violence, Peace, and Peace Research." *Journal of Peace Research* 6 (3): 167–191. https://doi.org/10.1177/002234336900600301.

Gerschenkron, Alexander. 1962. *Economic Backwardness in Historical Perspective: A Book of Essays*. Cambridge, MA: Belknap Press of Harvard University Press.

Ghanea, Nazila. 2015. *Driving while Bahá'í: A Typology of Religious Discrimination*. Equal Rights Trust. https://www.equalrightstrust.org/sites/www.equalrightstrust.org/files/ertdocs/Ghanea.pdf.

Hana Human Rights Organization. 2022. *Increased Pressure on Bahá'í Citizens in Sanandaj and Kurdish Regions*. https://hana-hr.org.

Herman, Thaddeus. 2019. *Crimes against Humanity: Iran and the Bahá'í Community*. https://www.academia.edu/download/58655500/Herman_Thaddeus_Crimes_Against_Humanity_Iran_and_the_Bahai_Community.pdf.

Huntington, Samuel P. 1968. *Political Order in Changing Societies*. New Haven: Yale University Press.

Iran Human Rights Documentation Center. 2007. *A Faith Denied: The Persecution of the Bahá'ís of Iran*. New Haven: Iran Human Rights Documentation Center. https://iranhrdc.org/a-faith-denied-the-persecution-of-the-bahais-of-iran.

Karlberg, Michael. 2010. "Constructive Resilience: The Bahá'í Response to Oppression." *Peace & Change* 35 (2): 222–257. https://doi.org/10.1111/j.1468-0130.2009.00627.x.

Kingston, Lindsey. 2015. "The Destruction of Identity: Cultural Genocide and Indigenous Peoples." *Global Dialogue* 17 (1): 377–389. https://doi.org/10.1080/14754835.2014.886951.

Levitsky, Steven, and Lucan A. Way. 2002. "The Rise of Competitive Authoritarianism." *Journal of Democracy* 13 (2): 51–65.

Mamdani, Mahmood. 2012. *Define and Rule: Native as Political Identity*. Cambridge, MA: Harvard University Press.

Manocha, Kishan, and Saba Tahzib. 2018. "Religion, Social Change and Responding to Persecution: The Case of the Bahá'í Community in Iran." In *Religion and Human Rights*, edited by John Witte and M. Christian Green. https://www.taylorfrancis.com/chapters/edit/10.4324/9781315595559-15.

Masumian, Adib. 2009. Debunking the Myths: Conspiracy Theories on the Genesis and Mission of the Bahá'í Faith. *Bahá'í Studies Review* 15: 79–95.

Milani, Shahin. 2016. Situation of the Bahá'í Minority in Iran and the Existing Legal Framework. *Journal of International Affairs*, June 6, 2016. https://jia.sipa.columbia.edu/news/situation-bahai-minority-iran-and-existing-legal-framework.

Momen, Moojan. 2025, November 6. "The Bábí–Bahá'í Revolution in Iran." In *Insights from the Field: Uncovering Early Bahá'í Contributions to 19th Century Iran*. Bahá'í World News Service.

Phillips, Nicola. 2017. "Power and Inequality in the Global Political Economy." *International Affairs* 93 (2): 429–444. https://doi.org/10.1093/ia/iix019.

Riazati, Naghmeh. 2011. "From Non-Recognition to Persecution: The Bahá'ís as the 'Monstrous Aliens' in the Islamic Republic of Iran." In *The Rights of Minorities in the Islamic State*.

Sanasarian, Eliz. 2000. *Religious Minorities in Iran*. Cambridge: Cambridge University Press.

Shabtab News. 2023. *Iranian Authorities Use Ankle Monitors to Track Bahá'í Detainees*. https://shabtabnews.com.

Shahvar, Soli. 2009. *The Forgotten Schools: The Bahá'ís and Modern Education in Iran, 1899–1934*. London: I.B. Tauris.

Smith, Peter. 2008. *An Introduction to the Bahá'í Faith*. Cambridge: Cambridge University Press.

UN General Assembly. 1966. *International Covenant on Civil and Political Rights*. https://www.ohchr.org/en/instruments-mechanisms/instruments/international-covenant-civil-and-political-rights

UN Human Rights Council. 2008. *Report of the Special Rapporteur on Freedom of Religion or Belief*. A/HRC/6/5/Add.4.

United Nations General Assembly. 2007. *Situation of Human Rights in the Islamic Republic of Iran*. New York: United Nations General Assembly Resolution, adopted 18 December 2007.

Weber, Max. 1978. *Economy and Society: An Outline of Interpretive Sociology*. Edited by Guenther Roth and Claus Wittich. Berkeley: University of California Press.

Zabihi-Moghaddam, Siyamak. 2021. "Religious Persecution of Bahá'ís under the Islamic Republic of Iran." In *Routledge Handbook of Religion and Human Rights*. https://www.taylorfrancis.com/chapters/edit/10.4324/9780429027772-46.

4 "Unyielding Voices"

Narratives of Bahá'í Women Post-Islamic Revolution

Introduction

While this chapter centers on the narratives of Bahá'í women and their expressions of agency and resilience in the aftermath of the Islamic Revolution, a scholarly analysis necessitates situating these experiences within their broader historical continuum. Any meaningful engagement with this subject would be incomplete without acknowledging the foundational role of Táhirih,[1] an iconic figure in both Iranian history and the early Bábí movement. To omit her would not only impoverish the discourse on women's resistance but also overlook a critical precedent in the theoretical understanding of female agency. Accordingly, the chapter opens with a brief examination of Táhirih's extraordinary acts of resilience and courage, as recorded in both Bahá'í sources and select Iranian historical accounts. Her enduring legacy serves as a vital lens through which to interpret the continued perseverance and resistance of Bahá'í women in contemporary Iran. Moreover, Táhirih's life and intellectual contributions offer a rare and invaluable case through which feminist studies, gender studies, and women's studies can reconsider the historical trajectories of women's agency in non-Western, religiously grounded contexts, thereby enriching broader minority studies by foregrounding how women within marginalized faith communities articulate autonomy, challenge patriarchal authority, and reshape possibilities for collective liberation.

1 Táhirih, born Fāṭima Baraghānī, was a pioneering nineteenth-century Iranian theologian, poet, and advocate for women's rights, renowned for her role within the Bābī movement – a precursor to the Bahá'í Faith. As the daughter of a prominent Muslim jurist, she received an extensive education in Islamic jurisprudence and theology, eventually emerging as one of the few female religious scholars of her time. Her intellectual authority and public resilience of gender norms positioned her as both a religious reformer and an early symbol of female emancipation in Iran.

Between June and July of 1848, over the course of approximately three weeks, a pivotal gathering of leading Bábí figures took place in the village of Badasht. This conference, organized in part and financially supported by Bahá'u'lláh, marked a decisive moment in the formal emergence and public assertion of the Bábí religion. Central to the proceedings were Táhirih and Quddús, whose theological and symbolic roles helped articulate a break from Islamic orthodoxy.

DOI: 10.4324/9781003567370-5

Prior to the Tobacco Revolt and the Constitutional Movement, one of the most significant socio-religious events of the Qajar period was the Badasht Conference of 1848. Often overlooked in broader narratives of modern Iranian history, the Badasht gathering, held in the summer of that year, brought together approximately 80 men and women, predominantly from educated and affluent backgrounds, to deliberate on the implications of the Báb's teachings and his anticipated release from incarceration (Moojan Momen 1983).[2] While the conference has frequently been interpreted as a religious event, a closer analysis reveals its profound sociopolitical and structural implications for the making of modern Iran.

The Badasht Conference not only signaled the emergence of a new religious discourse but also served as a performative space where early Bábí adherents, especially women, actively challenged the established norms of gender, religion, and authority. The event marked the first documented instance in Iranian society where men and women convened in a formal setting to engage in collective deliberation (Momen 1983), a direct result of the egalitarian spirit embedded in the Bábí teachings. This departure from the segregated and hierarchical norms of Shia Islamic society can be understood as a critical manifestation of agency, wherein individuals enacted their capacity to challenge dominant power structures through new modes of belief and social organization. Further, the participants' declaration of the Bábí Faith as independent from Islam was not merely theological but deeply political. It constituted an open agency against the religious orthodoxy and the sociopolitical foundations of Qajar Iran, which were tied to Shia Islam. Such agency, rooted in belief and identity, can be analyzed as a form of resilience, the capacity of individuals and communities to endure systemic repression while generating new collective imaginaries, as history also indicates.

Perhaps the most emblematic moment of the Badasht Conference, and indeed of early Bábí resistance, was Táhirih's unveiled appearance before a gathering of men. This act constituted a radical break with prevailing religious and cultural norms, revolutionary in both its symbolic and material dimensions. Drawing on eschatological readings of the Qur'an and the revelatory teachings of the Báb, Táhirih's unveiling was not merely a personal assertion of autonomy; it was a profound act of historical rupture (Brookshaw and Fazel 2008). It signified the termination of a religious epoch governed by hierarchical patriarchy and the inauguration of a new spiritual dispensation predicated on renewal, egalitarianism, and gendered emancipation.

2 Between June and July of 1848, over the course of approximately three weeks, a pivotal gathering of leading Bábí figures took place in the village of Badasht. This conference, organized in part and financially supported by Bahá'u'lláh, marked a decisive moment in the formal emergence and public assertion of the Bábí religion. Central to the proceedings were Táhirih and Quddús, whose theological and symbolic roles helped articulate a break from Islamic orthodoxy.

Táhirih's gesture, amplified by her standing as a respected scholar, poet, and teacher, redefined the boundaries of permissible female agency in nineteenth-century Iran. In doing so, she not only disrupted dominant gender ideologies but also reimagined the role of women as active agents in religious and national transformation. Her actions exemplify how deeply internalized belief systems can become potent instruments of both personal empowerment and collective transformation, what Mahmood (2005) refers to as "the politics of piety." Similarly, Butler's concept of performativity underscores how Táhirih's unveiling destabilized normative femininity by embodying a new configuration of religious and gendered identity (Butler 2009b). In this light, the Badasht Conference emerges not merely as a theological milestone but as a critical juncture in Iranian history, one where resilience and belief intersected to catalyze both personal liberation and communal transformation. Thus, the actions of Táhirih and her contemporaries illuminate how internalized theological commitments, when enacted in public and performative ways, can initiate enduring shifts in consciousness and institutional structures. These moments expose the potential of faith-based agency to challenge patriarchal theocracy and to lay conceptual foundations for future movements of reform and resistance.

Ten Bahá'í Women Executed in Shiraz, 1983

The narratives of the ten Bahá'í women executed in Shiraz in June 1983 offer critical insight into the dynamics of faith-based agency in the face of state-sponsored repression. Ranging in age from 17 to 54, these women exhibited extraordinary moral fortitude and spiritual conviction, resisting sustained efforts by the Islamic Republic to compel religious recantation. Analyzed through the dual frameworks of agency and resilience, their testimonies reflect more than passive endurance; they constitute deliberate, conscious enactments of faith-based identity and agency under conditions of coercive power. In refusing to renounce their beliefs, these women articulated a form of resistance that transcended political protest and entered the realm of ontological resilience, anchored in belief, sustained by community, and expressed through unwavering fidelity to principle. The narratives of these women, teachers, students, professionals, and homemakers, were united by a shared commitment to the Bahá'í principle of service to humanity as explored in depth in Chapter 2. Within this spiritual framework, acts of service emerge as expressions of faith-based agency and moral resilience, embodied practices through which individuals reclaim dignity, assert meaning, and resist dehumanization in the face of systemic oppression.

This section examines agency and resilience with a focus on Bahá'í women who were executed, imprisoned, or suffered the loss of loved ones through execution or enforced disappearance. It argues that their agency is rooted not only in personal or political resolve but in their religious identity, challenging secular and Western-centric models of agency. By tracing how these women construct resilient identities in the face of state-sponsored persecution, the section reframes repression not as silencing but as a catalyst for spiritual strength and collective empowerment. To explore these dynamics, the central research question guiding interviews with the families of the ten executed Bahá'í women was intentionally open-ended, allowing space for narrative complexity and emotional nuance. Archival materials and family testimonies, preserved across existing secondary literature, reveal a consistent inquiry posed to relatives: "Can you describe Miss [Name], and how she responded to her imprisonment and the death sentence issued by the Islamic court?" This open-ended prompt sought to elicit reflections on character, faith, and responses to state violence, rather than limiting women's experiences to acts of victimization. A synthesized account of these testimonies, drawn from diverse sources, follows in the next section.

Miss Simin Saberi, born on 2 March 1958 in Dehbid, Fars Province, came from a family of diverse religious backgrounds, Muslim and Jewish,[3] who independently embraced the Bahá'í Faith. A member of the Bahá'í Education Committee in Shiraz, Simin was known for her courage and clarity during interrogations. She was calmly refuting accusations and correcting misinformation about the Bahá'í Faith while answering the questions of interrogators. A fellow prisoner described her as consistently cheerful and spiritually radiant, even under pressure. Simin believed that by engaging with her interrogators, she might educate them about the true, apolitical nature of the Bahá'í Faith. At the time of her execution, Simin was 24 years old and was deeply concerned about comforting her grieving parents (Universal House of Justice 1986).

Mrs. Tahirih Arjumandi Siyavushi, a nurse and active member of the Bahá'í administrative order, was dismissed from her job due to her faith but continued working in a private hospital. Following her arrest, she endured solitary confinement and severe psychological pressure. When shown her

3 A person becomes a Bahá'í by recognizing Bahá'u'lláh as the Manifestation of God for this age and expressing the desire to be part of the Bahá'í community. Embracing the Bahá'í Faith does not require rejection or denouncement of one's previous religious background; rather, it affirms the divine origin of all major world religions. This principle, known as progressive revelation, acknowledges that figures such as Moses, Jesus, Muhammad, Buddha, and others were Manifestations of God who brought guidance suited to the needs of their time. https://www.bahai.org/beliefs/life-spirit/devotion/becoming-bahai

Regarding marriage, the Bahá'í Faith welcomes unions between individuals of different religions. Marriage is considered a sacred bond that requires the free and willing consent of both parties, as well as the approval of all living parents, to promote unity between families. A Bahá'í may marry someone of another faith, provided that both respect each other's beliefs and the spiritual purpose of marriage as a fortress for well-being and unity. https://www.bahai.org/beliefs/life-society/family-life/marriage

husband,[4] brutally tortured and close to death, as a tactic to force her to recant, Tahirih displayed remarkable emotional strength. Her resilience is further evident in her final encounter with her father, where she laughed and proclaimed, "Look how beautiful I am," shortly before her execution. A Bahá'í friend who had been imprisoned with her, and was later released, shared that Tahirih often urged her to leave Iran and speak out to the world about the suffering of Bahá'í prisoners and the injustices they endured at the hands of their oppressors. Tahirih also left a message for the Bahá'ís: "Tell the Bahá'ís, too, so they will completely detach themselves from material things, not be happy with the glitter and illusions of this contingent world, and devote their lives to service of the Cause" (Universal House of Justice 1986, 181).

Miss Akhtar Sabet Sarvestany, born in 1958 in Sarvestan, was a dedicated student and nurse, remembered for her humility, generosity, and unwavering commitment to serving others.[5] After being displaced from her hometown due to targeted attacks,[6] she continued her education in Shiraz and secured employment in a hospital. Upon her arrest on 23 October 1982, hospital authorities appealed for her release due to her valuable skills. However, she was told her freedom depended on renouncing her faith, an offer she declined. While in prison, she exercised a form of embodied agency by continuing to care for fellow inmates, including non-Bahá'í women, and applying her medical training to save lives. Her response to the threat of execution, "I hope so, by the grace of God" (Universal House of Justice 1986, 182).

Mrs. Nosrat Ghofrani Yaldai, well-known as a pillar of the Bahá'í community in Shiraz, was renowned for her hospitality and dedication to the faith. Her home functioned as a center for Bahá'í gatherings and education. When the police ordered her to stop hosting Bahá'í gatherings in her home, she refused, stating that "it was her religious obligation to be hospitable and to open her doors to friends and strangers alike" (Universal House of Justice 1986, 183). Her resistance escalated following her arrest in October 1982 alongside her son. Subjected to severe torture, including over 200 lashes, she was also pressured to publicly renounce her faith on state media. Nosrat firmly rejected their demand, declaring,

> I am but a drop compared to the ocean of the Cause of Bahá'u'lláh. Do you think you can stop the sun from shining? Was I a member of the Bahá'í Assembly when this religion was founded? You must

4 Jamshid Siavashi.

5 "Humility, kindness of heart, respect for her elders and an eagerness to serve others were among her distinguishing characteristics. While attending school she had to accept employment in order to assist her family. She was always attractively attired in simple and becoming clothes that she made herself" (The Universal House of Justice 1983, 182).

6 "She and her family and a large number of Bahá'ís had to abandon their homes when the enemies launched an attack in Sarvestan" (The Universal House of Justice 1983, 182).

understand that the light of the Cause of God will not vanish, even if I and others were to recant.

(p. 183)

Her son Bahram, along with five other Bahá'í men, was hanged two days before his mother. He faced the execution order with dignity and courage.[7]

Shirin Dalvand, born in Shiraz in December 1956, was an outstanding student at the University of Shiraz. Her senior thesis received exceptional praise, reflecting not only her academic talent but also her deep engagement with knowledge production despite her marginalized position (Universal House of Justice 1986). After her parents left for England, Shirin chose to remain in Shiraz, continuing her service on Bahá'í committees. Despite being under surveillance, she frequently visited the families of imprisoned and martyred Bahá'ís, offering them support and solidarity.

During her trial, when asked whether she was willing to die for her beliefs, Shirin responded calmly, affirming her readiness and expressing her hope for divine support in remaining steadfast. A fellow prisoner recounted Shirin's reflection on her birthday, noting that while her mother had gifted her a dress the previous year, "this year her gift was to be a prisoner for Bahá'u'lláh" (Universal House of Justice 1986, 176).

Despite repeated arrests, **Izzat Janami Ishraqi** and her daughter **Roya Ishraghi** chose to remain in Shiraz, steadfastly dedicating themselves to serving the local Bahá'í community. Following the revolution, their family's financial resources were targeted, the father's pension revoked, but their home became a refuge for displaced Bahá'ís (Universal House of Justice 1986). In one interrogation, Izzat, blindfolded and mocked by her interrogator, countered sharply: "I am just outwardly blind, but you are inwardly blind"[8]

7 Bahram Yaldaie, an assistant professor at Pahlavi University, was among the six Bahá'í men who did not choose Islam when faced with the question of "Islam or execution" and were hanged in Shiraz's Chogan Circle on the morning of 16 June 1983. The execution of these citizens was a continuation of the unprecedented pressure that the Islamic Republic had started against the Bahá'í community of this city. The other five men were Enayatollah Eshraghi, a retired employee of the National Oil Company (the father of Roya and husband of Izzat Janami); Bahram Afnan, a cardiologist; Jamshid Siavashi (husband of Tahirih Arjumandi), a shopkeeper; Abdol-Hossein Azadi, a veterinarian; and Kurosh Haqbeen, an electronics technician. https://iranpresswatch.org/post/23785/the-execution-of-six-bahai-men-in-june-1983-islam-or-the-hangmans-noose/

8 An eyewitness reported about the conditions of these ten women in prison: guards considered Bahá'ís as unclean therefore they would blindfold the Bahá'í prisoners, "give them the end of a folded newspaper; the other end of which they hold in their hand, and lead them to the interrogation room. In the interrogation room the blindfolded prisoners were made to sit down next to and facing the wall. Then the blindfold was removed and each prisoner was given a file containing questions which must be answered either in writing or verbally without turning around" (p. 184). The responses often produce insult on the part of interrogators who by every means would humiliate the Bahá'í prisoners.

(p. 177), which exemplifies an act of discursive agency that subverts the interrogator's intended humiliation. Rather than internalizing the powerlessness imposed by interrogation and physical disability, she reclaims moral and spiritual authority, reframing her condition as a source of insight rather than deficiency.

Roya, a veterinary student expelled for her religious identity, was known for her radiant personality and physical strength, especially her love for mountain climbing. Her sister Rozita's visit to prison after their father's execution marked another intimate moment of resilience. Roya, upon hearing the news, simply said, "Thanks God," indicating both grief and gratitude, while her mother responded with calm foresight: "I knew, I knew, I knew" (p. 177). Later, during a court interrogation, Roya was offered her father's reinstated pension and freedom for a simple recantation. Her response was resolute: "I will not exchange my faith for the whole world" (p. 178).

Zarrin Moghimi-Abyanih, a graduate in English literature from the University of Tehran, was denied the right to teach due to her faith. Instead, she worked in a petrochemical plant near Shiraz. When the judge threatened her life, she responded, "Even then that heart will cry out 'Bahá'u'lláh!" (Universal House of Justice 1986, 179).

Mahshid Niroomand, a physics graduate from Shiraz University, faced humiliation from an interrogator with no formal education. Yet she retained her self-respect, offering support to other prisoners and remaining composed during her trial. Her final declaration, "I have found the path to divine reality and I am not prepared to abandon it" (Universal House of Justice 1986, 180).

Miss Mona Mahodnezhad was a schoolgirl and the youngest of this group of martyrs who became a symbol of this group and her martyrdom was greatly publicized. She was born in 1965 in Yemen, where her parents were pioneering. The family returned to Iran in 1969 when the Government of Yemen expelled all foreigners. Despite being only 17 years old, Mona had already begun to articulate a thoughtful critique of systemic discrimination. In 1981, she wrote an essay asserting that "the fruit of Islam is freedom of conscience and liberty," a reflection of her early political consciousness (Universal House of Justice 1986). Following her arrest, she endured torture, beaten and forced to walk on her bleeding feet (Akhavan 2017), yet reportedly remained mentally centered. She was imprisoned at the same time as both her mother and father. After some time, her mother was released, but she remained in prison when her father was executed. It was during this period that Mona, Roya, Izzat, Tahereh, and Nosrat received the devastating news of the execution of their father, husband, or son, just two days before they themselves were hanged. According to a prison guard, Mona requested to be the last executed so she could pray for the others, and kissed the executioner's hand, saying, "In the Bahá'í Faith . . . we are only allowed to kiss the hands of those who kill us for our beliefs" (Universal House of Justice 1986, 179).

These narratives demonstrate that although each woman endured interrogation and trial in isolation, without knowledge of how others might respond, their independently articulated yet strikingly parallel expressions of moral courage reveal a shared ethical horizon. This unspoken convergence reflects a form of faith-grounded agency that transcended physical separation, evidencing the coherence of their spiritual commitments and the resilience of their moral vision. Together, these accounts provide a powerful lens for analyzing the intersection of spiritual conviction, epistemic agency, and sociopolitical resistance. In doing so, they challenge dominant secular paradigms that overlook how dignity, service, and religious identity can constitute potent forms of resistance. Their words and actions exemplify what Kristie Dotson (2011) terms *epistemic agency*: the assertion of one's right to produce and transmit knowledge even under conditions of systematic silencing.

To further unpack these layered expressions of agency and resistance, this study identifies five interrelated analytical dimensions.

1. Epistemic Agency and Counter-Discursive Resistance

   This dimension examines how acts of knowledge production and truth-telling operate as modes of resilience against hegemonic narratives. Simin's calm, articulate responses during interrogation disrupted the coercive logic of the state, transforming a punitive encounter into an occasion for ethical instruction. Similarly, Shirin's academic excellence and her decision to remain in Shiraz to serve the Bahá'í community reflect sustained intellectual integrity and moral clarity despite systemic exclusion. These actions resonate with postcolonial feminist epistemologies (Spivak 1988; Mohanty 1988), which defend the right of marginalized subjects to speak, theorize, and be heard. Within authoritarian contexts, such epistemic agency directly challenges the state's monopoly on truth, enacting forms of resistance that are at once intellectual and spiritual.

2. Testimonial Politics and Memory as Resistance

   This dimension explores how personal and collective memory shape political subjectivity and counteract erasure. The narratives of Tahirih and Mona illustrate the transformative potential of testimonial politics. Tahirih's appeals for global awareness and her call for spiritual detachment highlight her use of memory and voice as deliberate tools of resistance. Likewise, Mona's essay on religious freedom, her request to be executed last in order to pray for the others, and her gesture of kissing her executioner's hand reconfigure violence into a moment of sacred witnessing. These acts echo Butler's (2009a) and Das's (2007) insights about the ethics of witnessing, where storytelling becomes an active political intervention. Their testimonies move beyond individual suffering, contributing to collective memory, memory activism, and broader global efforts toward recognition and justice.

3. Embodied and Service-Oriented Agency

   Here, the focus is on how acts of service and embodied presence become forms of ethical resistance. Akhtar's quiet care for fellow prisoners, Bahá'í and non-Bahá'í alike, and her refusal to renounce her faith even at the threshold of execution exemplify embodied moral agency. Her actions articulate a subversive moral economy of care that destabilizes the logic of state violence. Similarly, Mahshid's composed response to humiliation and her steadfast solidarity with other prisoners demonstrate how ethical service can itself be a form of resistance. These narratives challenge conventional assumptions that resistance must be overt or confrontational, revealing instead the transformative political potential of relational, ethical, and service-oriented resilience.
4. Faith-Based and Intergenerational Resilience

   This dimension highlights how spiritual concepts, practices, and familial ties generate enduring forms of strength. The stories of Nosrat and her son Bahram, Izzat and her daughter Roya, and Mona and her parents illuminate how faith-based values shape intergenerational modes of resistance. Nosrat's metaphor, "I am but a drop compared to the ocean of the Cause of Bahá'u'lláh," situates her suffering within a larger spiritual cosmology, reframing disempowerment as purposeful sacrifice. Izzat's rhetorical strength and Roya's refusal to recant reflect a shared spiritual and moral framework carried across generations. Their final words, Roya's quiet "Thank God" and Izzat's resolute "I knew," signal a form of resilience grounded not in denial of suffering but in its integration into a meaningful spiritual narrative. Together, these familial ties illustrate a cultural infrastructure of resistance sustained by community and faith.
5. Youthful Conviction and Existential Autonomy

   The final dimension examines how younger women asserted moral agency and existential purpose despite intense repression. As the youngest among the executed women, Mona exemplifies the interplay of youthful conviction and interpretive autonomy. Her early critique of religious discrimination and her spiritual composure under torture testify to a precocious and deeply grounded sense of purpose. Her final acts transform the execution chamber into a site of sacred resistance. Similarly, Zarrin's philosophical confrontation with her judge, culminating in her declaration, "Even then that heart will cry out 'Bahá'u'lláh!'", embodies existential autonomy in the face of annihilation. These narratives contest entrenched stereotypes of female passivity, revealing how spiritual conviction can generate profound forms of moral resolve and political agency.

The deaths of these ten Bahá'í women unsettle conventional readings of execution as the extinguishing of agency. Viewed through the five analytical dimensions explored in this chapter, epistemic, testimonial, embodied, intergenerational, and existential, their actions illuminate a mode of resistance rooted in spiritual conviction rather than liberal individualism. Their refusal to recant, their ethical comportment under interrogation, and their practices of care and solidarity constitute a form of agency produced through faith, relationality, and moral intentionality.

Drawing on Butler's theorization of performativity under constraint, their speech, bearing, and collective coherence re-signify the execution chamber, converting a site of sovereign violence into a space where alternative ethical worlds are momentarily enacted. In this sense, their resistance is not reactive but world-constituting: it affirms a spiritual ontology that counters the state's epistemic and biopolitical erasures. By foregrounding how non-secular subjectivities generate resilient forms of political and ethical agency, their example broadens feminist theoretical vocabularies and challenges assumptions that read spirituality as incompatible with resistance. Ultimately, their narratives reveal how faith-grounded modes of knowing, remembering, serving, and meaning-making can articulate a potent counter-sovereign politics even in the face of imminent annihilation.

Faith in Fire

The life story of Shikar Nesa, an elderly Bahá'í woman from a small village near Birjand in post-revolutionary Iran, offers a powerful example of gendered resistance and faith-based resilience in the face of religious persecution. In 1980, during a wave of anti-Bahá'í violence, her home was attacked by a group of men while her husband was away. Upon resisting and pleading for her husband's safety, she was tied to a heavy wooden door with a nylon rope, doused with kerosene, and set on fire (Sears 1982b). By a twist of fate, the heat melted the nylon rope, allowing her partial escape, although she sustained severe burns. Emerging from the flames, she found only her husband's overcoat, later discovering his burned body discarded in a ditch.[9] Despite her injuries and trauma, the villagers, frozen by fear of the Islamic authorities, refused to assist her. She returned alone to her home, locked herself in, and was later found in a coma by her son-in-law. She passed away six days later. Her attackers were never arrested.

Shikar Nesa's story exemplifies embodied and service-oriented agency in the face of profound marginalization. As an elderly Bahá'í woman in a remote village, her acts of resistance, pleading for her husband, enduring torture, and surviving a brutal attack, move beyond institutionalized forms of power,

9 Mohammad-Hosein Masoumi was in the barn at the time of the attack. They beat him with a pickaxe, and left several sharp blows on his head, and then him set on fire and threw into a ditch. While this took place, Shekkar-Nisa Masoumi was held captive in their home by one of the attackers. https://iranbahaipersecution.bic.org/archive/shikkar-nisa-masoumi-murdered-nuk-khorasan-23rd-november-1980

foregrounding what Spivak (1988) describes as the subaltern's limited but potent means of enunciation. Her refusal to flee and her willingness to endure physical suffering constitute an embodied assertion of dignity, resonating with Butler's (1997) conception of performative agency, wherein vulnerability itself becomes a site of resistance. At the same time, her care for her husband and community aligns with feminist ethics of care (Tronto 1993), reframing nurturing labor as a political act rather than a private or apolitical gesture. The impunity of her attackers and the silence of her community reveal the gendered structure of violence, yet as Saba Mahmood (2005) argues in her study of women's piety movements, such silence does not necessarily denote passivity but can instead amplify the significance of embodied moral conviction. Shikar Nesa's life and death thus disrupt dominant narratives of women's passivity in contexts of religious and gendered persecution, demonstrating how marginalized women enact resistance through everyday acts of courage, faith, and steadfast care that are simultaneously spiritual and political.

Bahereh Motlagh and Her Daughters

The lived experiences of Bahereh Motlagh and her daughters, Afsaneh and Rozita Habibi, provide a compelling lens through which to examine the interrelated concepts of agency and resistance within the sociopolitical landscape of post-revolutionary Iran during its first decade. Their life narratives illuminate how Bahá'í women have navigated, endured, and actively resisted systemic state oppression. At the heart of their story are the traumatic events of 1980, when seven prominent Bahá'í men from the city of Hamadan, including Bahereh's husband, and the father and uncle of Afsaneh and Rozita, were arrested, subjected to brutal torture, and ultimately killed in prison.[10] This section foregrounds the gendered dimensions of agency and resistance, particularly as enacted by women responding to the violent loss of their loved ones within a repressive regime.

Maternal Agency

The family's response to the arrests and eventual execution of their male relatives illustrates a profound form of everyday resistance. The act of accompanying their children to prison visits, maintaining composure, and fostering

10 Following the verdict of the Islamic Revolutionary Court of Justice – Hamadan, seven individuals were sentenced to execution. The names of the executed individuals are as follows: Firouz Naiemi, Mohammad-Bagher Habibi, Naser Vafaie, Hosein Khandel, Mohammad Habibi, Hosein Motlagh Arani, Tarazollah Khozein. https://iranbahaipersecution.bic.org/archive/seven-bahais-executed-hamadan

hope through prayer became symbolic acts of resilience.[11] Afsaneh and Rozita recall that, during a prison visit, one of the younger children began to cry. When asked by the others why she was crying, she responded, "No, I'm not crying! The rays of the sun bother my eyes" (Rahimi 2011, 64). The young girl's effort to suppress her emotions, reflecting her mother's stoic composure, illustrates the early internalization of a moral framework of endurance – an embodied form of agency that functions not merely as behavior, but as a subtle mode of active resistance transmitted matrilineally. Another key recollection involves the regular prison visits on Mondays, when Bahá'í families would gather outside the prison gates in the hope of being granted access. Often denied entry or subjected to psychological torment, the mothers would ask their children to pray while they negotiated with prison authorities. "Please continue your prayer," they would say, "the door will be opened if you pray" (Rahimi 2011, 65). Even when their petitions were rejected, the act of praying became a collective, hopeful resistance, a faith-based agency of the state's attempt to sever familial and communal ties.

Afsaneh further recalled how, despite the harrowing conditions of incarceration, the seven Bahá'í men maintained a semblance of self-respect and order. In their cramped cell, they had carefully cleaned and arranged their space. During visits, they offered fruit, biscuits, and tea to their families, performing hospitality. They joked about their circumstances and shared handmade crafts, gifts that extended their sense of purpose beyond the prison walls. A Muslim prisoner, moved by their conduct, volunteered to smuggle letters written by one of the seven Bahá'í detainees, Afsaneh's father, out of the prison, fully aware of the risks involved (Rahimi 2011, 66–68). These letters reported the brutal interrogation practices and affirmed their unwavering commitment to their faith.

The moment of loss was particularly poignant for Afsaneh, who, upon hearing of her father's execution, turned to her mother and asked: "What happened?" Her mother responded with composed finality: "Everything is finished" (Rahimi 2011, 66). When Afsaneh questioned the meaning of her words, Bahereh reminded her of the intense hug her father had given her during their last visit. "Your father knew it was the last time he could hold you," she said. This maternal reframing of loss, interpreting death not as senseless tragedy but as a sacrifice rooted in faith, exemplifies the emotional labor women performed to sustain resilience within their families. In recontextualizing grief as part of a spiritual narrative, Bahereh shielded her daughter from

11 The seven families often traveled together to visit their loved ones in prison or to attend proceedings at the Islamic court in pursuit of updates on their cases. Similar patterns of collective support and shared struggle are also evident in the life experiences of other Bahá'í women who faced comparable circumstances.

despair while embedding meaning in suffering, thus performing a vital role in the intergenerational transmission of hope, dignity, and moral clarity.

Bahereh's agency extended beyond the domestic sphere. After the execution of the seven Bahá'í men, she and other Bahá'í women assumed leadership positions within the local Bahá'í administrative bodies, stepping into the very roles vacated by their imprisoned husbands. While they themselves were under state surveillance and emotional duress, they continued to serve their community, organize educational activities for Bahá'í youth expelled from schools, and advocate for justice – even approaching Islamic courts to challenge the persecution (Rahimi 2011, 73). Bahereh's most visible act of resistance occurred when she was informed that the bodies of the executed Bahá'ís had been delivered to a local hospital. Describing the scene in the morgue, a dark, blood-stained room where the injured corpses were stacked on top of one another, she expressed both horror and pride.

> One of my neighbors called me and said that one of the nurses who worked in Imam Khomeini Hospital, had called her and said that in early morning some soldiers brought some dead bodies from prison, maybe they were Bahá'í prisoners. Inform their families to come and take them. It was around 10 am. I went to the hospital and searched for the lifeless bodies. A watchman took me to a dark and dirty room. The lifeless bodies of our dear ones were fallen on top of each other while they were full of dried blood. Their clothes were torn and their bodies were tortured in a barbaric way. One of them had a whole in his belly, two hands of another one seemed to have been pressed by a press machine, the legs of another one was torn and the back of a next one was burned by iron. I couldn't hold my tears; I cried and said loudly O Bahaullah.
>
> Then I came out of the room and went to the open yard of the hospital. There were many people who asked me what happened to them. They could see the bodies from the broken window, but they couldn't believe what they saw. Why they were killed like that? I explained to them that they were Bahá'ís and because they didn't recant their faith they were killed. I said: "you must know them; they served you for many years as a teacher, lawyer, and doctor. Did they do anything wrong to you? Their crime was their faith; truthfulness and serving people, nothing else." The watchmen of the hospital came to me and said: "you are in danger, the agents of the government are around you, please be quiet and stop talking." I thanked him but I couldn't be silent, again I started talking to people, I replied to the questions.
>
> (p. 72–76)

Bahereh's act of public mourning, standing in the hospital courtyard to name the executed Bahá'ís and affirm their faith, constitutes a powerful instance of faith-based testimony and performative resistance. Despite warnings from hospital staff and the presence of government agents, her refusal to remain silent and her declaration, "You must know them; they served you for many years," reclaims the narrative from the regime and asserts the ethical legitimacy of the victims. This act exemplifies Butler's notion of performativity under constraint, where speech and bodily presence, even under coercive power, retain the capacity to re-signify meaning and disrupt dominant narratives. Bahereh's voice, in a space marked by surveillance and fear, transforms the hospital courtyard into a site of moral clarity and public witness.

The burial ceremony became another site of collective agency. Afsaneh described how the broken ambulance carrying the corpses moved slowly through the city, trailed by a large crowd of both Bahá'í and Muslim residents. Initially, Bahá'í prayers filled the air; then, Muslim participants began chanting their own prayers, and eventually, all voices united in the cry of *"Yā Bahā'u'l-Abhá"* (O Glory of the Most Glorious, a Bahá'í prayer) (Rahimi 2011). In that moment, the burial was transformed into an interfaith protest, a shared expression of grief and resistance. State agents were present, taking photos, yet remained silent in the face of the emotional intensity of the scene. The symbolic power of this funeral procession was not lost on Afsaneh. Despite her initial desire to avoid the sight of her mother and others in their grief, she eventually resolved to serve the mourners who came to their home the following day. She prepared tea and sweets, welcomed guests, and upheld the Bahá'í tradition of hospitality. Her ability to transform personal suffering into communal service reflects a mature expression of agency that had been cultivated through years of observing her mother and other Bahá'í women's strength.

The funeral procession described by Afsaneh further illustrates collective and interfaith agency. As Bahá'í and Muslim prayers converged in a shared cry of *"Yā Bahā'u'l-Abhá,"* the burial became a symbolic protest against religious persecution. Despite the presence of state agents, the emotional unity of the mourners rendered oppression visible yet powerless. Afsaneh's decision to serve the mourners the next day, preparing tea and sweets in line with Bahá'í traditions, reflects a service-oriented ethic rooted in resilience. Her actions, shaped by years of observing Bahereh and other Bahá'í women, demonstrate the intergenerational transmission of moral clarity and hope. These intimate gestures of care and conviction challenge erasure and foster social transformation. Their story exemplifies how faith-based agency, cultivated through everyday acts of courage and care, can redefine political subjectivity and resist hegemonic silencing.

The Case of Kamelia Abadi's Mother

The life story of Kamelia Abadi illustrates the profound spiritual resilience and embodied agency of Bahá'í women under systemic persecution in post-revolutionary Iran. The Islamic Republic's strategy of targeting Bahá'í mothers, misusing kinship ties to compel them to recant their faith, reflects a patriarchal logic that equates motherhood with ideological malleability. Yet the narrative shared by Kamelia disrupts this logic by highlighting a form of resistance grounded not in overt political agency but in moral and spiritual steadfastness. After the execution of her mother, Kamelia discovered years later that her infant brother, born in prison, had been taken by the Islamic court and placed with a Muslim family. Eighteen years after leaving Iran, now living in the United States, she was contacted by this very brother.

> I knew that my mother was pregnant because one day from the prison she called me and said that you have a brother, but I didn't know that the Islamic court gave my brother to a Muslim family after executing my mother. I came out of Iran after few years but always remember my dear mother and whenever I remember that how much she was in pain and suffered in prison, my tears come down. When I moved to USA, I became familiar with some Bahá'ís and after studying some Bahá'í books accepted the faith. Almost 18 years after I left Iran, one night my phone rang and a man called me: "my dear sister."

The voice of the young man said how he found my phone number and introduced himself as son of my mother, who was born in prison. I started crying and said,

> "I know you are my brother because our mother called me when you were born in prison and told me that I have a brother." Then he explained that when he was 14 years old he understood that he is not the real son for that family and when he asked Muslim mother, she explained that the Islamic court had gave him to her. He said: "my mother was very kind to me and she helped me to find my real mother's family. They gave me some contact numbers which helped me to find you." He was in tears and said that though he is a Muslim but he is proud of her mother, because she gave her life for her faith.
>
> (Rahimi 2011, 280–286)

The life story of Kamelia and her mother offers a compelling illustration of faith-based and intergenerational resilience, as well as embodied and testimonial agency, in the context of systemic persecution of Bahá'í women in post-revolutionary Iran. Her mother's execution and the forced adoption of her infant brother by a Muslim family reflect the Islamic Republic's strategy of weaponizing kinship and motherhood to suppress religious identity. Yet this attempt at ideological erasure failed to sever the spiritual and emotional bonds that persisted across time and geography. Kamelia's eventual acceptance of the Bahá'í Faith after immigrating to the United States, and her brother's search for his origins, reveal how faith and memory endure, transmitted through maternal sacrifice and familial remembrance. This narrative exemplifies what Butler (2004) describes as agency under constraint, where resistance is enacted not through liberal autonomy but through moral clarity and spiritual steadfastness in the face of coercive power.

The emotional reunion between siblings, facilitated by the Muslim adoptive family's support, underscores the ripple effects of sacrificial agency, extending beyond the Bahá'í community to affect the moral consciousness of others. Kamelia's mother's refusal to recant her faith, even under threat of death and separation, challenges the state's control over both religious identity and familial structures. Her body, as a site of suffering and defiance, embodies what Oliver (2001) terms witnessing as ethical response, where testimony restores intersubjective recognition in contexts of dehumanization. The retelling of this story functions as testimonial resistance, preserving suppressed histories and contributing to a collective archive of Bahá'í endurance. Rather than weakening the community, the regime's persecution catalyzed a form of communal resilience, where intimate acts of care, remembrance, and spiritual conviction become powerful tools of resistance and social transformation.

Afagh Rahimian Embodied Agency of Care

Afagh, the wife of executed Bahá'í prisoner Rahim Rahimian, passed away in 2023, leaving behind a life defined not only by profound loss but by enduring faith-based agency. Her story unfolds across decades of religious persecution, state-sanctioned violence, and intergenerational resilience in the Islamic Republic of Iran. While her husband was executed in 1984 for his Bahá'í Faith, with his body likely interred in an unmarked grave in Khavaran Cemetery, Afagh was left to care for their sons, Kamran and Keyvan,[12] amidst the confiscation of all family assets and the loss of their home. Rather than leave Iran, she chose to remain, anchoring her children through a life of steadfast conviction and maternal resilience. She raised her sons to become advocates of peace and confidence. Kamran Rahimian became a pioneer in introducing nonviolent communication (NVC) in Iran, inspired by the teachings of Marshall Rosenberg. Alongside Keyvan and other family members, he promoted the practice across the country through workshops, literature, and digital content.

Afagh's agency extended beyond her household. When her sons and daughters-in-law were repeatedly imprisoned for teaching in the Bahá'í Institute for Higher Education (BIHE), an underground university for Bahá'í youth barred from Iranian academia, Afagh became the primary caregiver for her grandchildren. In 2013, while her son Keyvan and daughter-in-law Faran Hesami were incarcerated, she raised Artin and Zhina (a 2-year-old grandson and a 12-year-old granddaughter) on her own. She navigated both

12 He has been arrested and imprisoned in Evin prison since 18 July 2023.

psychological hardship and bureaucratic injustice, regularly visiting courts and officials to advocate for her family's basic rights, a quiet act of resistance demonstrating significant female agency in constrained contexts. In one of her public statements, she detailed the strict limitations of prison visitation: only minutes behind glass, and brief physical contact permitted between her grandson and his imprisoned mother, Faran. Regarding Faran's condition and her visits with her child, Afagh stated, "She is in good physical health. Her child and I visit her weekly. I am allowed only five or six minutes behind glass, but the child is permitted limited physical contact with her in the visiting hall. I sit and watch, cherishing those brief moments of mother and son together." With the school year approaching, Afagh recounted their request for a temporary leave for Faran during Shahrivar [September] so she could accompany her child on his first day of school. When authorities denied Afagh pleaded persistently, stating, "This child (Artin) was only two when both his parents were arrested. He is now seven, starting school, and still, they would not agree. But I have not given up; I will keep trying."

Afagh's life exemplifies a quiet yet profound architecture of resistance, best understood through the lenses of faith-based and intergenerational resilience, embodied and service-oriented agency, and everyday resistance. Her decision to remain in Iran after her husband's execution and her lifelong commitment to raising her children and grandchildren in the Bahá'í Faith reflect a deep-rooted spiritual endurance. This maternal resilience, sustained through asset confiscation, imprisonment of her children, and bureaucratic injustice, illustrates what Ungar (2008) defines as relational resilience, the determination to preserve familial bonds under structural oppression. Her caregiving labor, advocacy in courtrooms, and emotional support for her family are acts of embodied resistance, challenging the state's attempt to fragment Bahá'í families and erase their presence. These gestures align with James C. Scott's (1985) theory of "everyday resistance," where moral courage is enacted through subtle, persistent acts in ordinary spaces such as visitation halls and burial negotiations.

Even in death, Afagh's story remained a site of political confrontation. Denied burial in Tehran's Bahá'í cemetery, her family offered her body to the Tehran University of Medical Sciences in honor of her devotion to learning. The university later withdrew under state pressure, resulting in her unauthorized burial in Khavaran without family consent. As her son Kamran recounted, "Afagh was laid to rest near our father . . . without our family in attendance." Yet her legacy endured. A letter from 14 women prisoners in Evin mourned her as one who resisted "injustice and violence" and defied "weakness and abjection." Her life challenges narratives of passive victimhood and reframes resistance as a continuum of care, memory, and moral clarity. Her sons' advocacy for peace and education in Iran further demonstrates the intergenerational transmission of ethical agency, transforming private suffering into civic engagement.

Conclusion: Rethinking Agency Through Bahá'í Women's Narratives

This chapter has examined the lived experiences and narrative testimonies of Bahá'í women in post-revolutionary Iran to theorize multiple, intersecting forms of agency – epistemic, discursive, intergenerational, interpretive, collective, relational, maternal, and sacrificial. Through their stories and practices, these women articulated modes of resistance grounded not solely in opposition to state power but in an internally cultivated commitment to justice, spiritual integrity, and human dignity. Their agency, therefore, is not reducible to liberal notions of autonomy or individual rupture; rather, it is rooted in a deeply embodied moral clarity informed by Bahá'í theological principles.

To unpack these complex expressions of resistance, this chapter analyzed ten life narratives across five interrelated dimensions of agency. First, epistemic agency and counter-discursive resistance illuminated how truth-telling, knowledge production, and spiritual testimony disrupted state-sanctioned erasures. Second, testimonial politics and memory as resistance demonstrated how personal and collective remembrance reclaimed histories otherwise rendered illegible within the Islamic Republic's ideological framework. Third, embodied and service-oriented agency revealed caregiving, ethical labor, and steadfast presence within hostile environments as enactments of moral defiance. Fourth, faith-based and intergenerational resilience highlighted the continuity of spiritual practices and values across generations despite systemic surveillance, discrimination, and violence. Finally, youthful conviction and existential autonomy illustrated how younger Bahá'í women mobilized moral clarity and purposeful action to navigate and contest oppressive sociopolitical conditions.

Taken together, these dimensions demonstrate that Bahá'í women's agency was not merely reactive but consciously cultivated within structures of belief and translated into everyday practices that sustained community life under persecution. From quiet resilience displayed in prison visiting rooms and dignified mourning enacted through burial rites, to the ethical care performed in classrooms, courtrooms, and private homes, these women transformed ostensibly passive spaces into potent arenas of moral and political resistance. Such acts resonate with James Scott's (1990) theorization of infrapolitics and Shirin Rai's (2008) conceptualization of resistance-as-performance, as well as with forms of embodied, faith-based resilience that unsettle authoritarian and patriarchal norms.

Central to this reframing is Maurice Hamington's (2004) notion of the "embodied agency of care," which redefines caregiving as a politically charged ethical practice rather than a retreat into domesticity. In the context of Bahá'í women's lived experiences, care becomes a site of resistance: raising children under surveillance, advocating in judicial spaces, and offering hospitality amidst state repression all emerge as acts of spiritual conviction and moral steadfastness. Their bodies function as vessels of ethical testimony, echoing Kelly Oliver's (2001) theory of witnessing as a relational practice that restores dignity within contexts of dehumanization.

By foregrounding these underexamined narratives, this chapter contributes to broader efforts to decolonize dominant understandings of agency and to expand feminist and political theory beyond secular frameworks (Mohanty 2003; Mahmood 2005). It challenges assumptions that equate agency exclusively with overt defiance, instead demonstrating how religious subjectivities and spiritual ethics can generate enduring forms of empowered action. The resilience of Bahá'í women thus emerges not as isolated acts of heroism but as a collective, intergenerational, and epistemic process of meaning-making and resistance. Their narratives not only record survival under conditions of persecution but also articulate an alternative vision of agency – spiritual, embodied, relational, and transformative – thereby redefining the possibilities of resistance within authoritarian and patriarchal contexts.

Reference List

AI-assisted tools, including Grammarly, were used for language editing and structural clarity. The author retained full responsibility for the intellectual content of the chapter.

Akhavan, Payam. 2017. *In Search of a Better World: A Human Rights Odyssey*. Toronto: House of Anansi Press.

Brookshaw, Dominic Parviz, and Seena B. Fazel, eds. 2008. *The Bahá'ís of Iran: Socio-Historical Studies*. New York: Routledge.

Butler, Judith. 1997. *Excitable Speech: A Politics of the Performative*. New York: Routledge.

Butler, Judith. 2004. *Undoing Gender*. New York: Routledge.

Butler, Judith. 2009a. *Frames of War: When Is Life Grievable?* London: Verso.

Butler, Judith. 2009b. "Performativity, Precarity and Sexual Politics." *AIBR: Revista de Antropología Iberoamericana* 4 (3): 47–60. https://doi.org/10.11156/aibr.040305.

Das, Veena. 2007. *Life and Words: Violence and the Descent into the Ordinary*. Berkeley: University of California Press.

Dotson, Kristie. 2011. "Tracking Epistemic Violence, Tracking Practices of Silencing." *Hypatia* 26 (2): 236–257. https://www.jstor.org/stable/23016544.

Hamington, Maurice. 2004. *Embodied Care: Jane Addams, Maurice Merleau-Ponty, and Feminist Ethics*. Urbana: University of Illinois Press.

Kelly Oliver. 2001. *Witnessing: Beyond Recognition*. Minneapolis: University of Minnesota Press.

Mahmood, Saba. 2005. *Politics of Piety: The Islamic Revival and the Feminist Subject*. Princeton, NJ: Princeton University Press.

Mohanty, Chandra Talpade. 1988. "Under Western Eyes: Feminist Scholarship and Colonial Discourses." *Feminist Review* 30 (1): 61–88. https://doi.org/10.2307/1395054.

Mohanty, Chandra Talpade. 2003. *Feminism without Borders: Decolonizing Theory, Practicing Solidarity*. Durham, NC: Duke University Press.

Momen, M. 1983. "The Social Basis of the Bábí Upheavals in Iran (1848–53): A Preliminary Analysis." *International Journal of Middle East Studies* 15 (2): 157–173.

Rahimi (Mottahedeh), Pouran. 2011. *Eshgh be Baha-ye Jan [عشق به بهای جان]*. USA: Baha'i National Center.

Rai, Shirin M. 2008. *The Gender Politics of Development: Essays in Hope and Despair*. London: Zed Books.

Scott, James C. 1985. *Weapons of the Weak: Everyday Forms of Peasant Resistance*. New Haven, CT: Yale University Press.

Scott, James C. 1990. *Domination and the Arts of Resistance: Hidden Transcripts*. New Haven, CT: Yale University Press.

Sears, William. 1982a. *Release the Sun: The Story of the Báb, the Prophet-Herald of the Bahá'í Faith*. Oxford: George Ronald.

Sears, William. 1982b. *The Flame: The Story of the Bahá'í Faith in Iran*. Oxford: George Ronald.

Spivak, Gayatri Chakravorty. 1988. "Can the Subaltern Speak?" In *Marxism and the Interpretation of Culture*, edited by Cary Nelson and Lawrence Grossberg, 271–313. Urbana and Chicago: University of Illinois Press.

Tronto, Joan C. 1993. *Moral Boundaries: A Political Argument for an Ethic of Care*. New York: Routledge. https://doi.org/10.4324/9781003070672.

Ungar, Michael. 2008. "Resilience across Cultures." *British Journal of Social Work* 38 (2): 218–235.

Universal House of Justice. 1986. *The Bahá'í World, Volume XIX: 1983–1986*. Haifa, Israel: Bahá'í World Centre.

5 Concluding Through Self-Reflection

Introduction

As this book reaches its conclusion, it does so at a moment of profound political and social upheaval in Iran, a conjuncture that lends renewed urgency to the arguments advanced throughout this volume. Recent military escalation involving Israel, supported by the United States, alongside prolonged and deliberate internet shutdowns imposed by the Iranian state, has not only rendered communication with those inside the country increasingly difficult but has also exposed the evolving logics of repression, exclusion, and control (Amnesty International 2026; NetBlocks 2026; United Nations Human Rights Council [UNHRC] 2026; Office of the United Nations High Commissioner for Human Rights 2026). These developments signal a critical transformation in the architecture of state power. While ethnic, religious, and political minorities have long been subjected to intensified surveillance and discrimination, the current moment reveals how mechanisms historically deployed against marginalized groups are now being extended to society at large. In this sense, repression in Iran has become increasingly generalized. Following the ceasefire, internet access was selectively restored only for a narrow circle of individuals deemed loyal to the regime, while the vast majority of the population remained digitally excluded (Access Now 2026; NetBlocks 2026). Even when limited access through VPNs later became possible, its prohibitive cost rendered it inaccessible to large segments of society.

The consequences of this digital deprivation have been profound and unevenly distributed. Entire sectors of employment dependent on online connectivity collapsed, disproportionately affecting women who had relied on home-based production, informal labor, and online entrepreneurship for economic survival. Students and researchers whose academic work depended on digital resources likewise experienced severe disruption (International Labour Organization 2025; UNESCO 2025). These conditions underscore that marginalization in contemporary Iran cannot be understood solely through fixed social categories such as ethnicity, religion, class, education, or wealth. Rather, marginality is increasingly produced through state practices that systematically exclude, incapacitate, and silence those perceived as threatening to ideological authority. What emerges, then, is an understanding of minority

DOI: 10.4324/9781003567370-6

status not as a static identity but as a politically imposed condition, one that can expand to encompass ever-wider segments of society. The state's capacity to manufacture exclusion through infrastructural control, economic deprivation, and surveillance demonstrates how authoritarian power continually redraws the boundaries of belonging and disposability.

From the vantage point of exile, this moment is apprehended not only analytically but also as lived reality. This reflection is offered not as anecdotal evidence, but as an illustration of how repression structures the very conditions under which knowledge is produced and sustained. Like many in the Iranian diaspora, I remain suspended in uncertainty, unable to confirm the safety of family members, friends, and colleagues. This enforced distance is intensified by generational and technological constraints: my elderly parents and immediate family lack safe access to global communication platforms, and any attempt to connect would expose them to heightened surveillance and risk due to my political history. As a result, we have been unable to remain in contact for months. This condition of imposed silence, produced through fear, technological restriction, and distance, brings into sharp relief the forms of precarity, vulnerability, and erasure that this book seeks to theorize. Repression operates not only through spectacular violence, but through the slow dismantling of livelihoods, social ties, and communicative possibility. The present moment thus renders visible the stakes of this analysis: how power governs through exclusion, how vulnerability is unevenly distributed, and how agency persists even under conditions designed to extinguish it.

Alongside deepening poverty, one of the most alarming developments has been the sharp escalation in arrests, executions, and state violence directed at individuals for acts as minimal as accessing the internet, participating in the January 2026 protests, or expressing dissent on social media, including liking or reposting content that diverges from official ideology. These punitive measures signal an intensification of authoritarian governance in which the boundary between political dissent and everyday life has effectively collapsed (Amnesty International 2026; Iran Human Rights Documentation Center 2026; Office of the United Nations High Commissioner for Human Rights 2026). These events should not be understood solely as violations of freedom of expression or human rights, grave as those violations are. They confirm one of this study's central claims: that forms of repression initially directed at specific minorities, such as the Bahá'í community, constitute broader technologies of rule that can be expanded to encompass society at large. What was once experienced as targeted persecution increasingly appears as a generalized condition of vulnerability, cutting across religious, ethnic, classed, and generational boundaries (Human Rights Watch 2026; UNHRC 2026). These dynamics also reverberate transnationally, as war, infrastructural deprivation, and political exclusion generate cascading effects beyond Iran's borders.

Against this backdrop, this chapter returns deliberately to the lives and testimonies of Bahá'í women who were executed, imprisoned, or otherwise subjected to systematic persecution after the 1979 Islamic Revolution. Across the preceding chapters, this book has sought to expand prevailing conceptualizations of gender agency, religious identity, and minority subjectivity under authoritarian rule. The narratives of these women, woven throughout the analytical arc of the volume, constitute a significant epistemological intervention, compelling a rethinking of how agency is recognized, inhabited, and theorized in contexts where repression operates through law, ideology, and everyday life. By placing the experiences of Bahá'í women in dialogue with the broader condition of Iranian society, this chapter advances a theoretical argument about the gendered logic of state power. Patriarchal interpretations of Sharīʿa that privilege male authority do not remain confined to regulating women's bodies or minority communities; they extend into the governance of the nation itself. In this framework, the state assumes a masculinized position of authority, while society is rendered feminized, expected to submit, internalize discipline, and face punishment for perceived disobedience.

Practices historically justified through the regulation of women's conduct, surveillance, coercion, moral discipline, and punitive correction, are now applied broadly across society. The repression of dissent and criminalization of deviation are no longer experienced solely by women or minorities but increasingly imposed upon the population as a whole. This shift underscores one of the book's central claims: that minority persecution functions as a testing ground for authoritarian governance, where techniques of domination are refined before being normalized. Read together, these dynamics raise a critical analytical question: how is agency lived and sustained under conditions where overt dissent is criminalized and everyday life becomes a site of surveillance? It is here that the narratives examined in this book acquire their full significance, not as exceptions to domination, but as alternative modes of political subjectivity forged within it.

Rather than conforming to secular liberal paradigms that equate resistance with overt defiance, these accounts of Bahá'í women demonstrate that agency also emerges through embodied, relational, and spiritually grounded practices. Acts of caregiving, teaching, service, and ethical steadfastness, often dismissed as private or apolitical, acquire insurgent meaning when performed under threat and exclusion. In such contexts, continuity itself becomes a mode of resistance. Across this book, trauma and loss appear not only as sources of suffering but as generative sites of moral and communal labor. Raising children in climates of fear, sustaining fragmented communities, and preserving histories the state seeks to erase function as acts of refusal and self-assertion. In environments designed to render certain lives disposable, caregiving and hope become quite yet potent forms of resistance.

These narratives resonate with Saba Mahmood's (2005) theorization of ethical self-formation, revealing agency as cultivated rather than oppositional, while also exposing the symbolic violence Judith Butler (2009) identifies in the production of "ungrievable" lives. By centering these experiences, the book documents not only violence but the ethical, affective, and epistemic repertoires through which marginalized women assert political subjectivity. The trajectory of this work has been shaped by the entanglement of scholarly inquiry and lived experience. My position as a Bahá'í woman, former prisoner of conscience, and human rights advocate living in exile has informed both the questions posed and the interpretive lenses employed. The Woman, Life, Freedom movement and subsequent waves of repression have further sharpened these reflections, demanding a reconsideration of how power, resistance, and belonging are conceptualized.

In closing, the book's central arguments come into sharper relief: that agency under repression requires expanded theoretical vocabularies; that the ethical and affective labor of marginalized women is politically consequential; and that attending to their narratives reshapes our understanding of political life under authoritarianism. To continue with dignity in contexts that insist on silence is itself a political act, and it is from such persistence that alternative futures continue to be imagined.

Integration Into a Broader Academic Argument

This chapter, situated within the broader architecture of the book, is grounded in a dual epistemological framework that places the analytical rigor of academic scholarship in sustained dialogue with the interpretive depth of Bahá'í spiritual thought. Rather than introducing new empirical material, it elaborates the theoretical implications of the study's findings, drawing out their conceptual and normative significance. Throughout the volume, Bahá'í writings are engaged not simply as sources of ethical guidance but as substantive ontological and epistemological interventions that open alternative horizons for understanding justice, service, hope, agency, resilience, and processes of social transformation. These texts are treated analytically rather than devotionally, for the conceptual work they perform under specific historical and political conditions. In this sense, the book aligns with what Leela Gandhi (2006) conceptualizes as a post-secular critique, one that unsettles the presumed separation between scholarly reason and spiritual knowledge and treats resilience as a relational and multidimensional praxis.

This orientation generates a productive tension that has shaped both the book's argument and my own intellectual trajectory. The political and spiritual ruptures that structure the lives of the women at the center of this study, and that have also marked my own life, continually challenge the epistemic frameworks through which social reality is interpreted. Academic methodology, with its emphasis on abstraction, critical distance, and empirical verification, often sits uneasily alongside the embodied, faith-informed epistemologies that animate Bahá'í thought. Rather than resolving this tension by privileging one mode of knowing over the other, this book advances a dialogical approach in which scholarly and spiritual traditions interrogate and enrich one another. This methodological hybridity expands the conceptual terrain through which resistance, agency, and political subjectivity can be understood, particularly in contexts where spiritual identity is inseparable from political repression and social struggle.

Within this framework, positionality operates not as a limitation but as a method. My role as both participant and observer is articulated through what I describe as critical witnessing, a mode of engagement that recognizes knowledge production as situated rather than detached. The structural violence experienced by the women whose testimonies anchor this study, surveillance, dispossession, and enforced invisibility, resonates with my own experiences of imprisonment, exile, and diasporic activism. Their resilience, grounded in ethical service, collective care, and spiritual coherence, offers a counter-narrative to authoritarian systems that seek to fragment, silence, and erase. This mode of witnessing foregrounds the ethical responsibility of scholarship to the communities whose lives and struggles it seeks to render intelligible, underscoring that interpretation itself is a political practice.

Seen through this lens, this chapter functions as both synthesis and theoretical intervention. It argues that the political imagination cultivated by Bahá'í women, shaped through solidarity, ethical commitment, and spiritual discipline, constitutes not merely a reaction to persecution, but a generative model of emancipatory possibility. Their practices of endurance foreground the political force of hope, the durability of embodied memory, and the often-unrecognized labor of care. Together, these practices invite a reorientation of political theory, redirecting analytical attention away from spectacles of confrontation toward the sustained forms of action through which life and meaning are preserved under conditions of erasure.

This claim, however, necessitates closer attention to how hope itself is theorized and enacted under conditions of repression. If hope is central to the political imagination articulated in these women's lives, it cannot be understood as abstract affect or future-oriented optimism, a formulation that has been critically interrogated in scholarship on affect and political desire (Berlant 2011; Bloch 1986). Rather, hope emerges here as a cultivated and collective practice, one that sustains ethical orientation and social continuity when the horizons of formal politics are systematically foreclosed, echoing anthropological and feminist accounts of ethical life and agency under constraint (Mahmood 2005; Das 2007).

It is at this juncture that Bahá'í discursive frameworks, particularly as articulated in contemporary institutional texts, offer an analytically productive lens. By conceptualizing hope as disciplined, relational, and historically grounded, these texts illuminate how marginalized communities transform endurance into forms of political agency that do not rely on confrontation or visibility, resonating with broader theories of non-liberal and quiet forms of political action (Bayat 2013). The discussion therefore turns to the 2026 Ridván message of the Universal House of Justice as a critical site through which this understanding of hope, agency, and resilience can be theoretically situated (Universal House of Justice 2026).[1]

1 "When the world's horizons darken, hope becomes a scarce and precious resource – but one with which the community of the Greatest Name has been richly blessed because of its conviction

Read together, the Ridván message and the narratives examined in this book underscore that hope, as articulated and enacted by the Bahá'í community in Iran, is not merely a thematic element of spiritual discourse but a mode of knowledge production and political orientation. The message does not simply describe resilience; it actively theorizes it, rendering ethical commitment, collective memory, and disciplined practice intelligible as sources of agency under repression. This convergence of spiritual articulation and political meaning points toward a broader methodological implication: if hope can function simultaneously as ethical practice, political capacity, and epistemic resource, then the analytical boundaries separating the spiritual from the scholarly, and experience from theory, must be reconsidered.

The epistemological hybridity that guides this work is therefore not only methodological but deeply political. It challenges entrenched binaries between the spiritual and the scholarly, the personal and the political, and the ethical and the analytical. By foregrounding the lived experiences of Bahá'í women as both subjects and producers of knowledge, this chapter interrogates dominant paradigms of resistance and reclaims spirituality as a legitimate site of critical inquiry and transformative possibility. In doing so, it gestures toward a reimagined scholarly praxis, one that is ethically accountable to the communities it engages, attentive to the moral dimensions of knowledge production, and capable of recognizing political insight where conventional theory often fails to look.

Concluding Reflections: Reframing Women's Agency Through the Bahá'í Experience in Iran

Taken together, the chapters of this book constitute a sustained theoretical intervention in feminist scholarship and broader debates on agency, resistance, and political subjectivity under authoritarian rule. Grounded in the lived experiences and testimonies of Bahá'í women in post-revolutionary Iran and informed by my own trajectory as a Bahá'í woman shaped by repression, imprisonment, and exile, the study brings embodied knowledge into critical dialogue with feminist and political theory. In doing so, it challenges prevailing analytical frameworks

---

about the future of humanity and because of what it has learned from its own experience. Multitudes yearn for the hope you can bring to their hearts.

For a golden example of a community that has long sheltered the flame of hope, we look to the wronged yet ever-patient, ever-steadfast, ever-resilient followers of Bahá'u'lláh in the Cradle of His Faith. See how disciplined they have remained, how committed to principle over decades of unrelenting oppression – and how resolved they have been to learn from the advances made by their fellow believers in other lands, how determined to serve and console their fellow citizens in their own land. To so many of their compatriots they have been, and continue to be, a beacon of hope, a fount of compassion and insight, and trusted companions on the path of service" (Universal House of Justice, *Riḍván Message 2026*, 2. Bahá'í Reference Library).

that privilege abstraction, visibility, and liberal epistemologies as the primary sites from which agency can be recognized and theorized.

Against dominant paradigms that equate agency with autonomy, overt dissent, or secular rationality, this book advances a feminist approach attuned to relational, embodied, and ethically grounded forms of political action. Drawing on intersectional feminism, post-colonial critique, and non-Western epistemologies, it demonstrates that agency under conditions of repression is not enacted through withdrawal from power or exceptional acts of defiance, but through sustained ethical engagement with constraining structures. Practices of care, education, service, and community building, often dismissed as private, apolitical, or adaptive, emerge here as consequential forms of political labor that preserve social meaning and continuity in contexts designed to erode them.

Central to this contribution is the reconceptualization of faith-based agency as both a methodological orientation and a theoretical intervention. Building on feminist scholarship on ethical self-formation, particularly Mahmood's critique of liberal agency, the book articulates a mode of political subjectivity that exceeds the binary of resistance and submission. Agency is shown to take shape through moral discipline, spiritual coherence, and intergenerational responsibility, expanding the feminist lexicon to include practices through which marginalized women cultivate durable forms of ethical life under conditions of surveillance, exclusion, and disposability. In this framework, political action is neither heroic nor oppositional by necessity, but cumulative, relational, and historically situated.

By tracing the multiple registers through which Bahá'í women enact agency, epistemic, testimonial, embodied, intergenerational, and existential, this study foregrounds how knowledge itself becomes a site of struggle. The concept developed here as the paradox of suppressed alternatives captures this dynamic: authoritarian repression seeks to erase not only dissenting subjects but the moral and social imaginaries they sustain, yet in doing so renders visible the enduring power of those alternatives as lived practices. Minority persecution thus emerges not as a marginal phenomenon, but as a critical analytic site for understanding how authoritarian power is tested, refined, and ultimately contested through everyday ethical labor.

Serving as both synthesis and theoretical positioning, this concluding intervention underscores a final claim that runs throughout the book: marginalized women are not only subjects of repression but producers of political theory. By sitting in a personal narrative alongside sustained conceptual analysis, the study demonstrates that lived experience is not supplementary to theory, but constitutive of it. At a historical moment marked by intensifying authoritarianism and shrinking civic and epistemic space, the frameworks developed here invite a reorientation of feminist and political theory, one that recognizes hope, care, and ethical endurance not as residues of powerlessness, but as generative sources of political imagination and transformative possibility.

Reference List

AI-assisted tools, including Grammarly, were used for language editing and structural clarity. The author retained full responsibility for the intellectual content of the chapter.

Access Now. 2026. *Iran: Internet Shutdowns, Digital Repression, and the Expansion of Surveillance during Conflict*. https://www.accessnow.org.

Amnesty International. 2026. *Iran: Escalating Repression, Internet Shutdowns, and the Criminalization of Dissent*. https://www.amnesty.org.

Bayat, Asef. 2013. *Life as Politics: How Ordinary People Change the Middle East*. 2nd ed. Stanford: Stanford University Press.

Berlant, Lauren. 2011. *Cruel Optimism*. Durham, NC: Duke University Press. https://doi.org/10.1215/9780822394716.

Bloch, Ernst. 1986. *The Principle of Hope*. Translated by Neville Plaice, Stephen Plaice, and Paul Knight. 3 vols. Cambridge, MA: MIT Press. Originally published 1954–1959.

Butler, Judith. 2009. *Frames of War: When Is Life Grievable?* London: Verso.

Das, Veena. 2007. *Life and Words: Violence and the Descent into the Ordinary*. Berkeley: University of California Press. https://doi.org/10.1525/9780520939530.

Gandhi, Leela. 2006. *Affective Communities: Anticolonial Thought, Fin-de-Siècle Radicalism, and the Politics of Friendship*. Durham, NC: Duke University Press.

Human Rights Watch. 2026. *World Report 2026: Iran*. New York: Human Rights Watch. https://www.hrw.org/world-report/2026/country-chapters/iran.

International Labour Organization. 2025. *Gendered Impacts of Digital Exclusion and Informal Labor in Crisis Contexts*. https://www.ilo.org.

Iran Human Rights Documentation Center. 2026. *Arrests, Executions, and Repression Following the January 2026 Protests*. https://iranhrdc.org.

Mahmood, Saba. 2005. *Politics of Piety: The Islamic Revival and the Feminist Subject*. Princeton, NJ: Princeton University Press.

NetBlocks. 2026. *Internet Disruptions in Iran during Military Escalation*. https://netblocks.org.

Office of the United Nations High Commissioner for Human Rights. 2026. *Iran: Human Rights Violations Linked to Protests and Online Expression*. https://www.ohchr.org.

UNESCO. 2025. *Education under Disruption: Digital Access and Inequality in Conflict Settings*. https://www.unesco.org.

United Nations Human Rights Council. 2026. *Report of the Special Rapporteur on the Situation of Human Rights in the Islamic Republic of Iran*. https://www.ohchr.org.

Universal House of Justice. 2026. *Riḍván Message to the Bahá'ís of the World*. Haifa: Bahá'í World Centre. https://www.bahai.org.

Index

For Product Safety Concerns and Information please contact our EU representative GPSR@taylorandfrancis.com Taylor & Francis Verlag GmbH, Kaufingerstraße 24, 80331 München, Germany